Welcome to *Brain Games*®: *Find the Cat Challenge!* Real cats can get into cabinets or sneak out through an open window, but no matter the setting, you'll find one hidden cat in each photo of this book. It's not just fun to search for a friendly furry familiar—it's good for your brain! Research suggests a varied routine of regular mental exercise can help keep your brain feeling and acting healthier. If you get stumped, check the answers in the back.

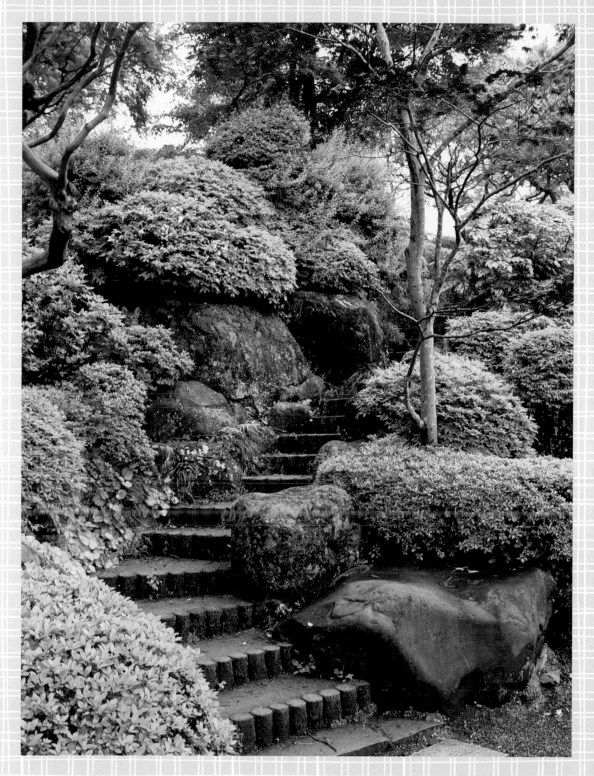

Answer on page 130.

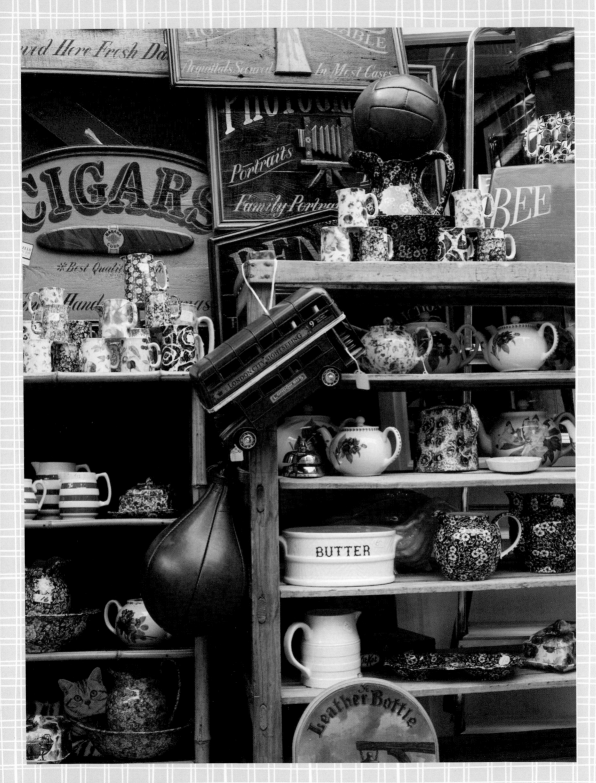

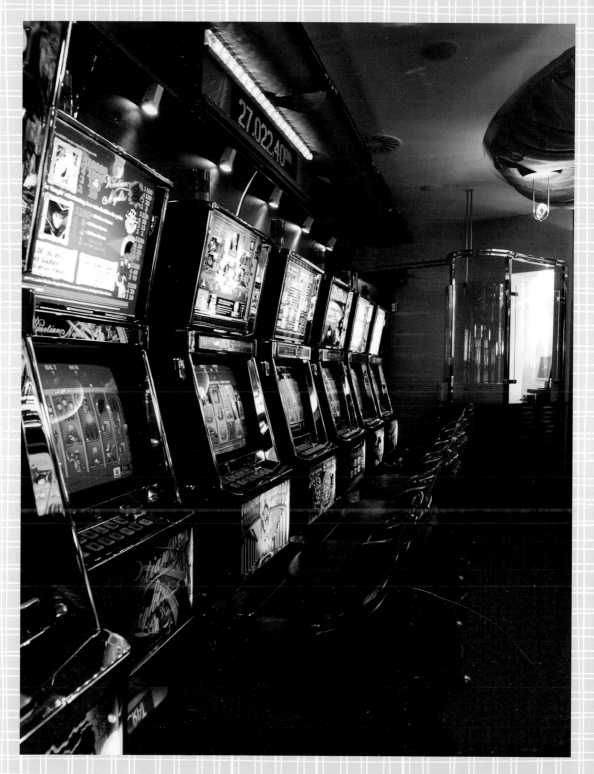

Answer on page 130.

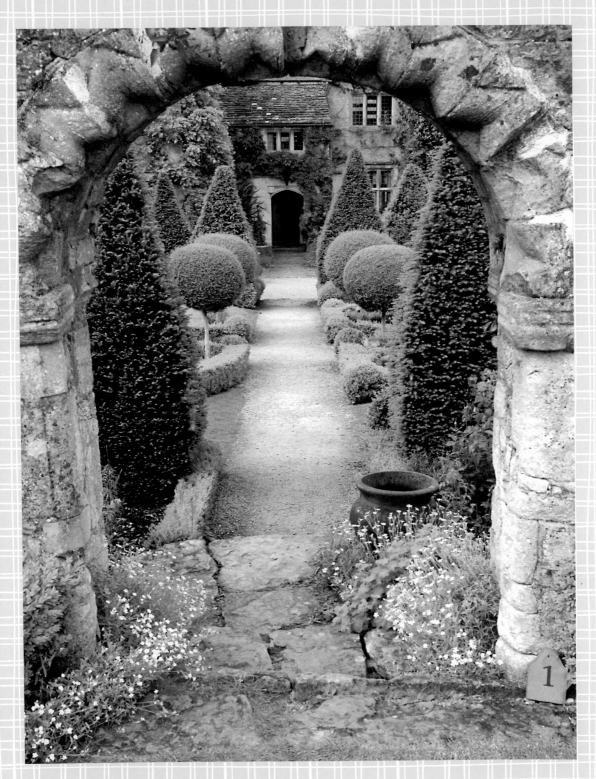

Answer on page 130.

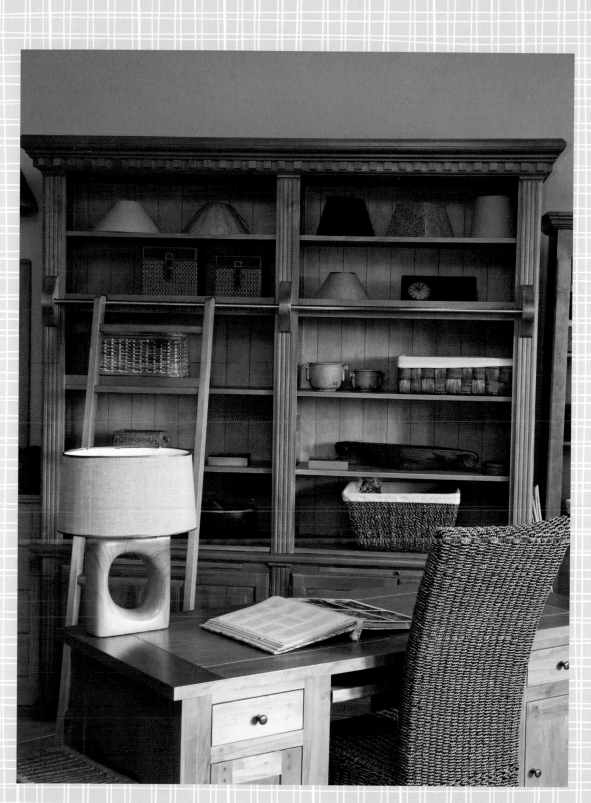

Answer on page 131.

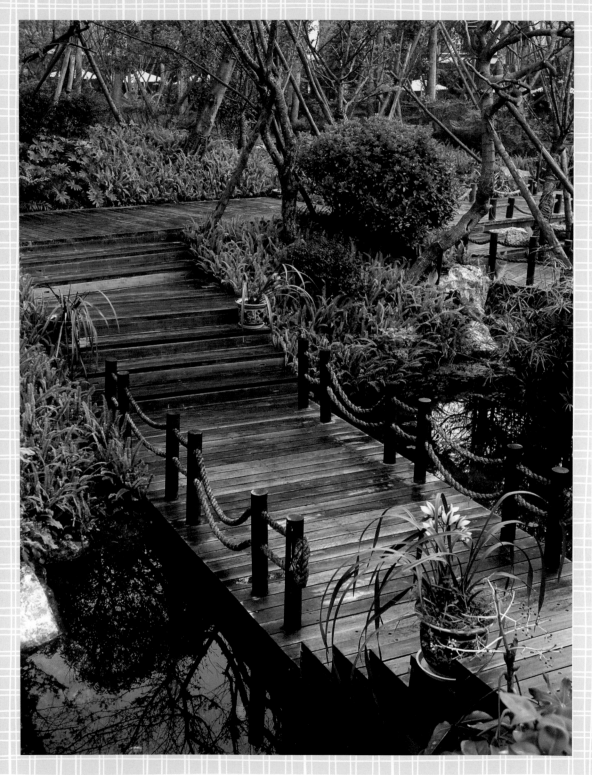

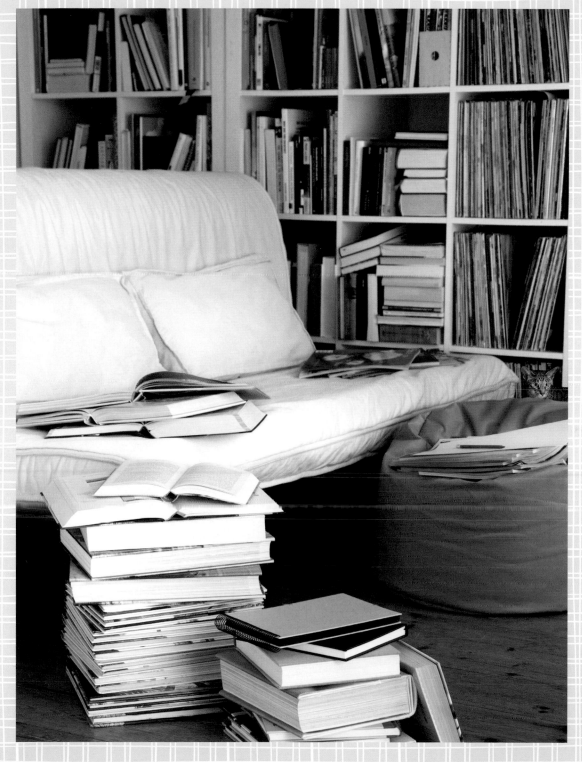

Answer on page 131.

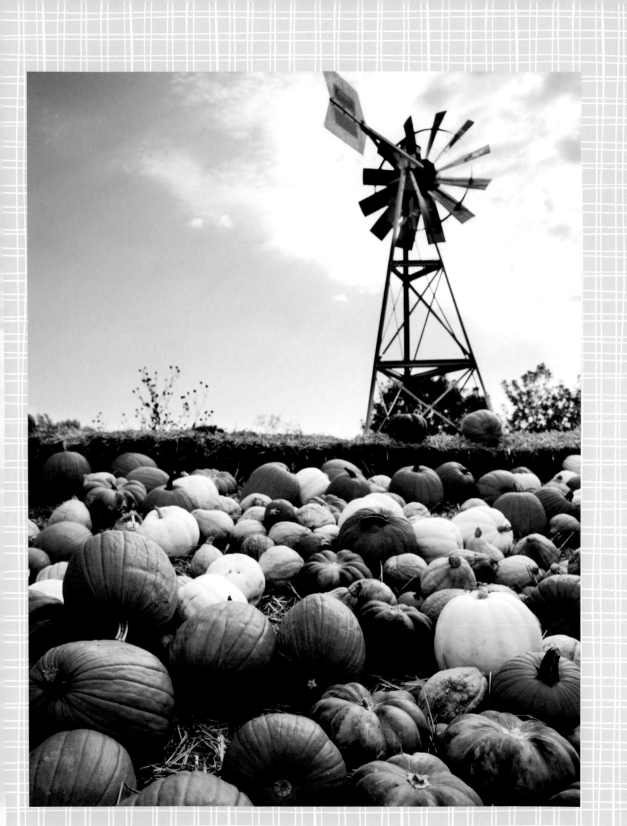

Answer on page 131.

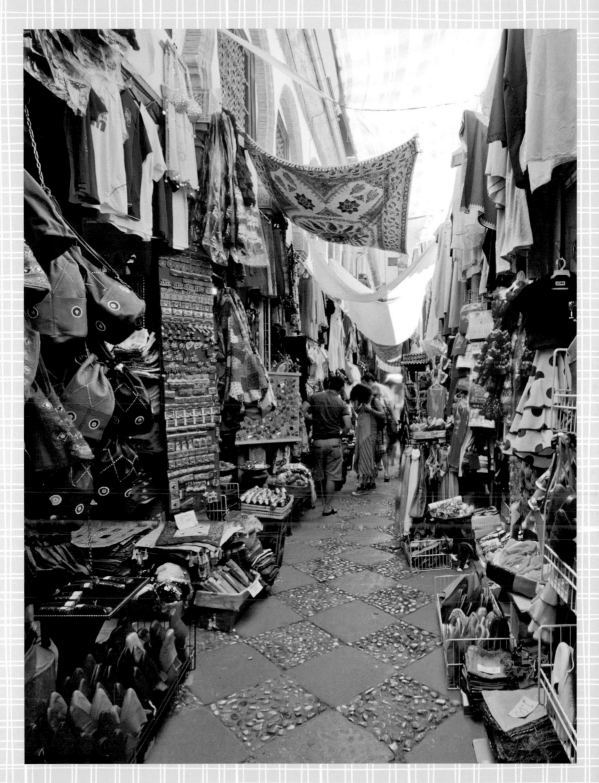

Answer on page 132.

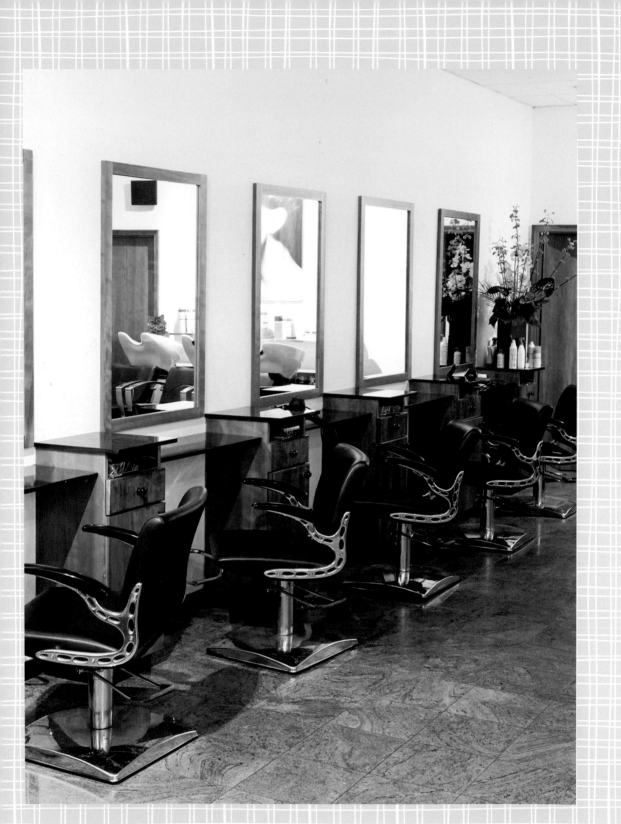

Answer on page 132.

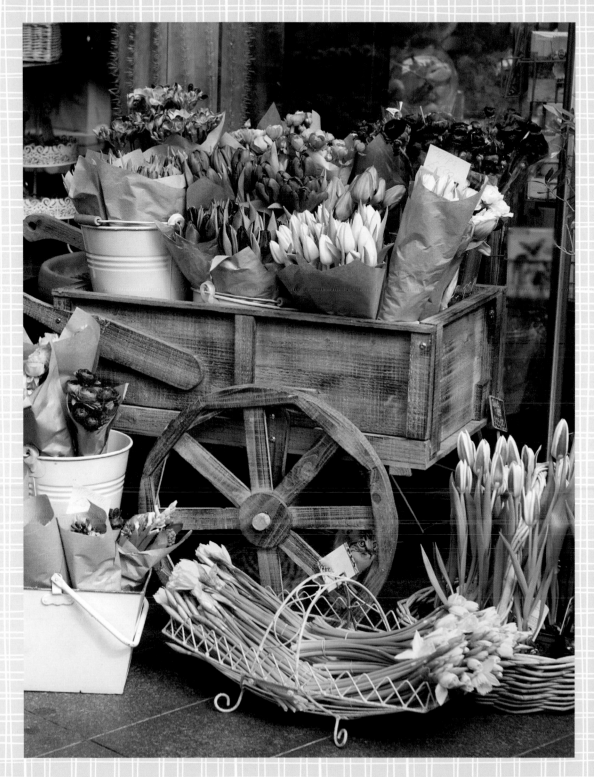

Answer on page 132.

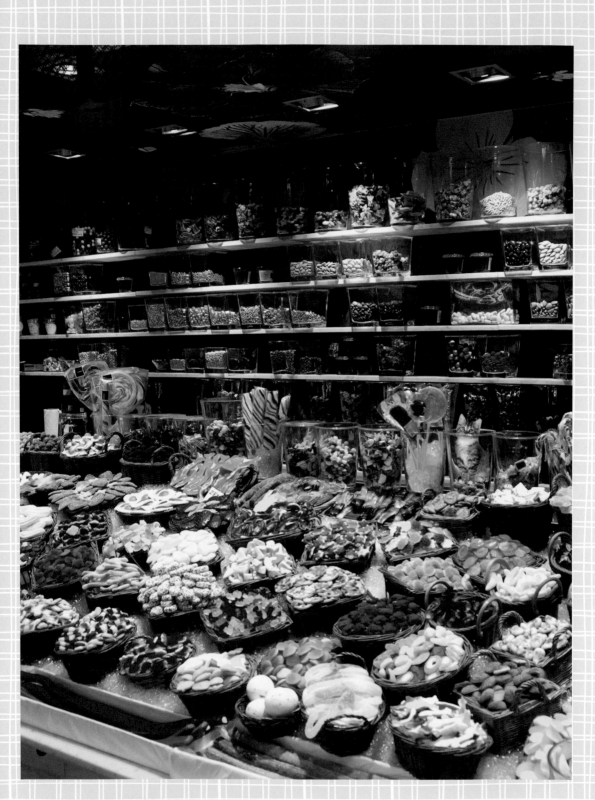

Answer on page 132.

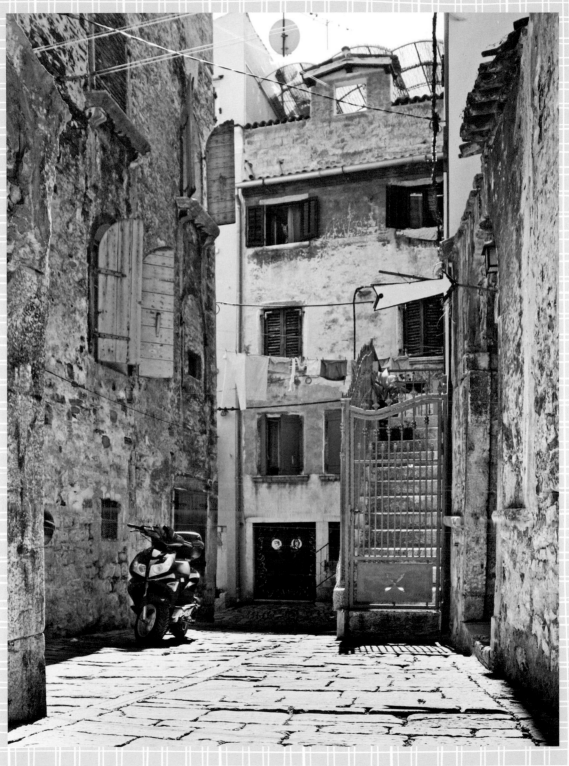

Answer on page 133.

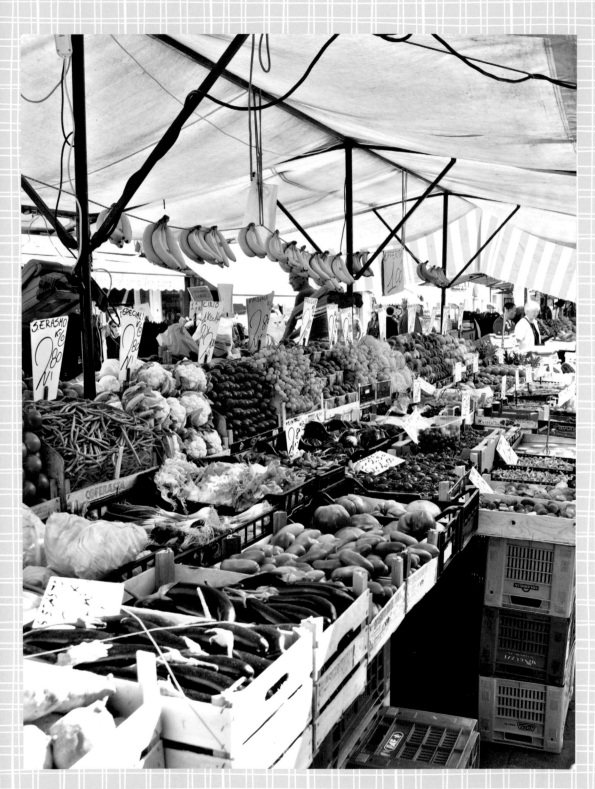

Answer on page 133.

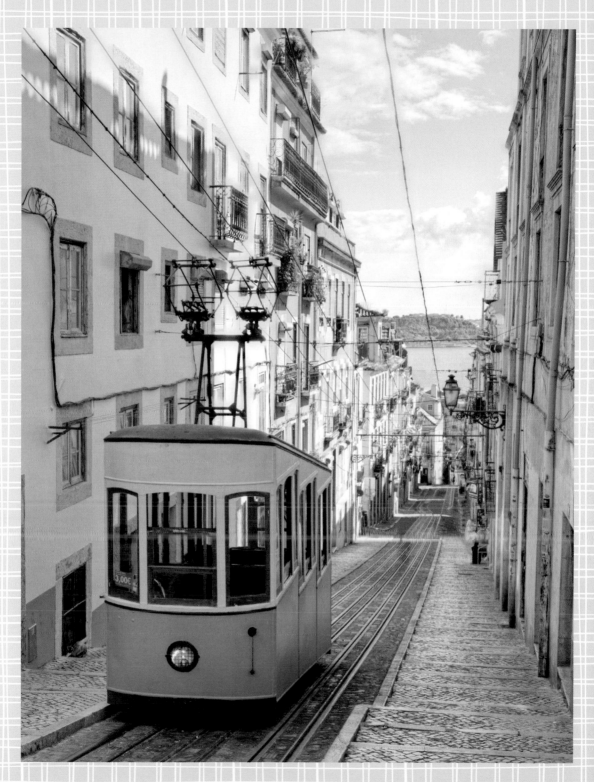

Answer on page 133.

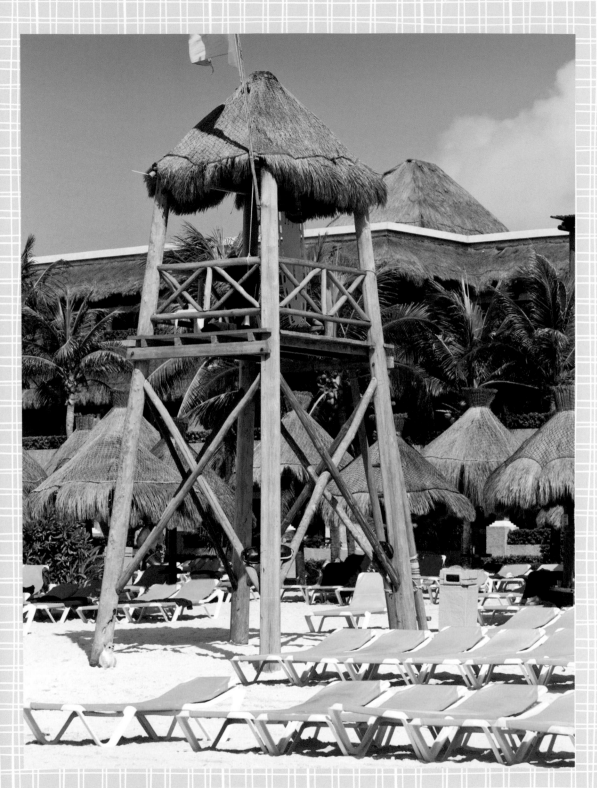

Answer on page 133.

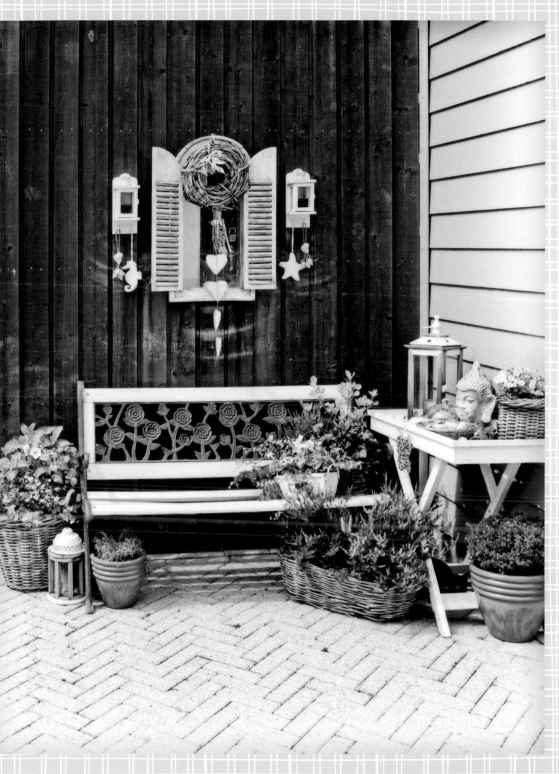

Answer on page 134.

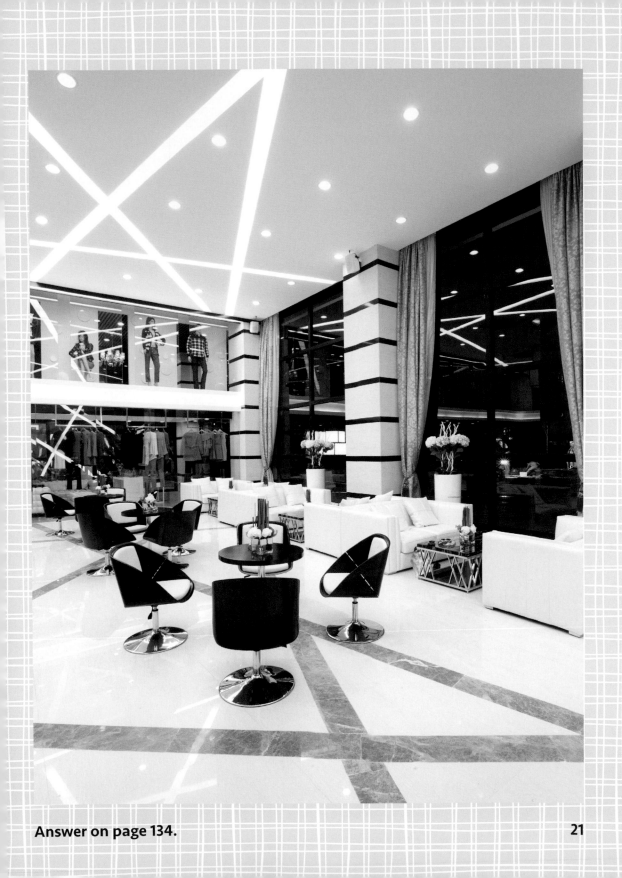

Answer on page 134.

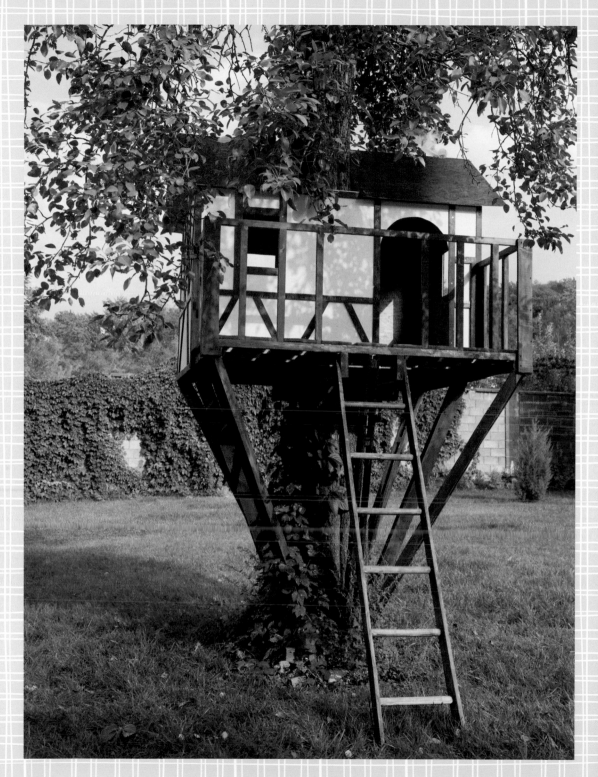

Answer on page 134.

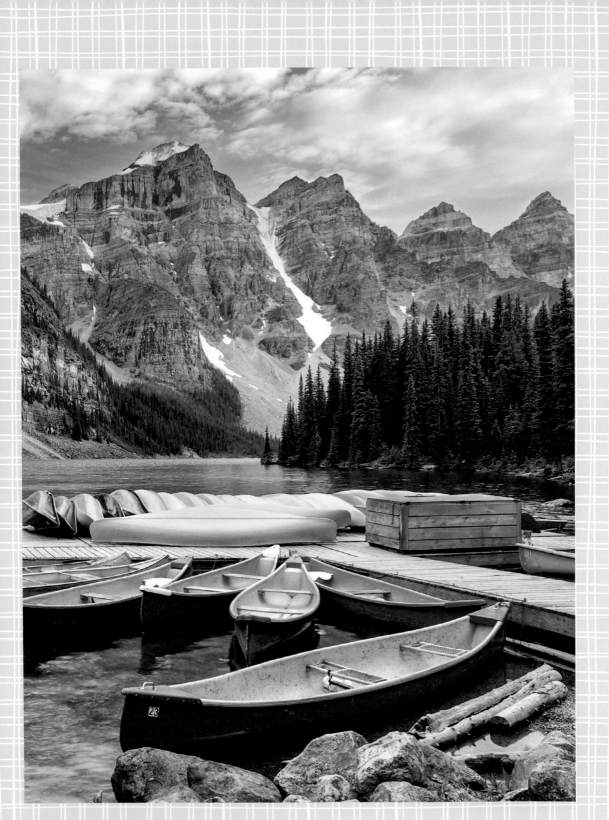

Answer on page 134.

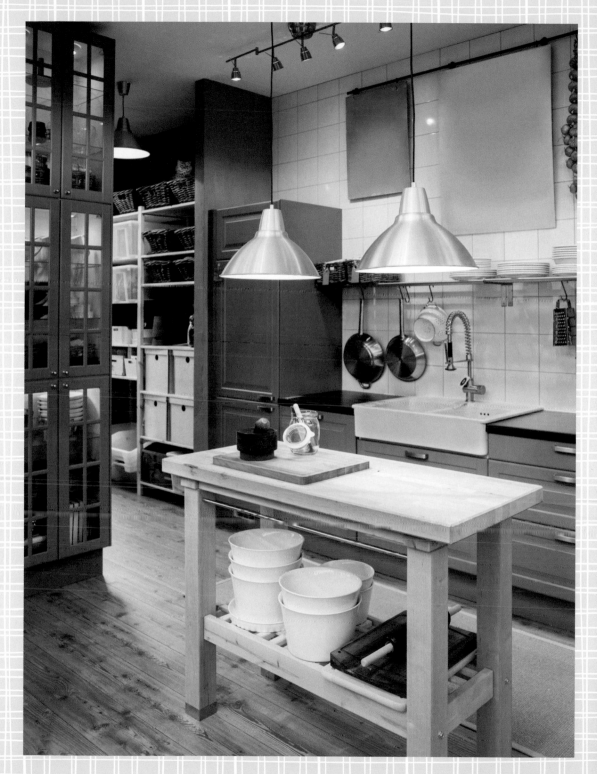

Answer on page 135.

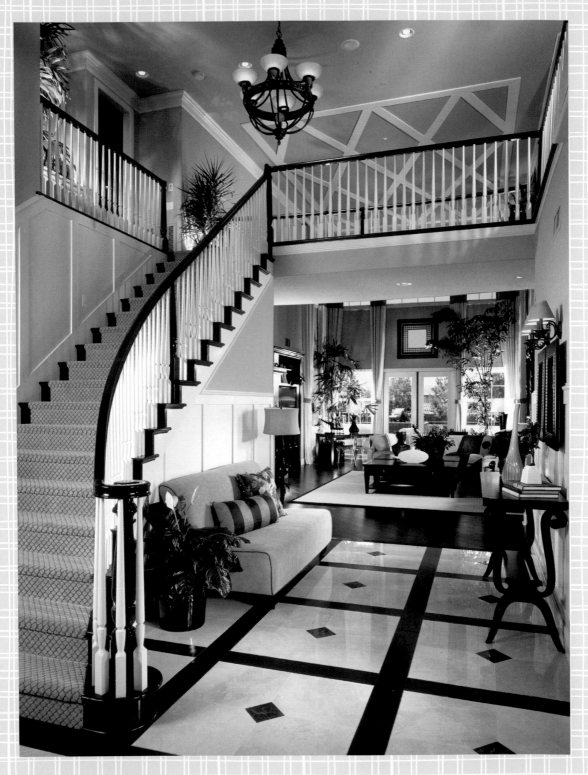

Answer on page 135.

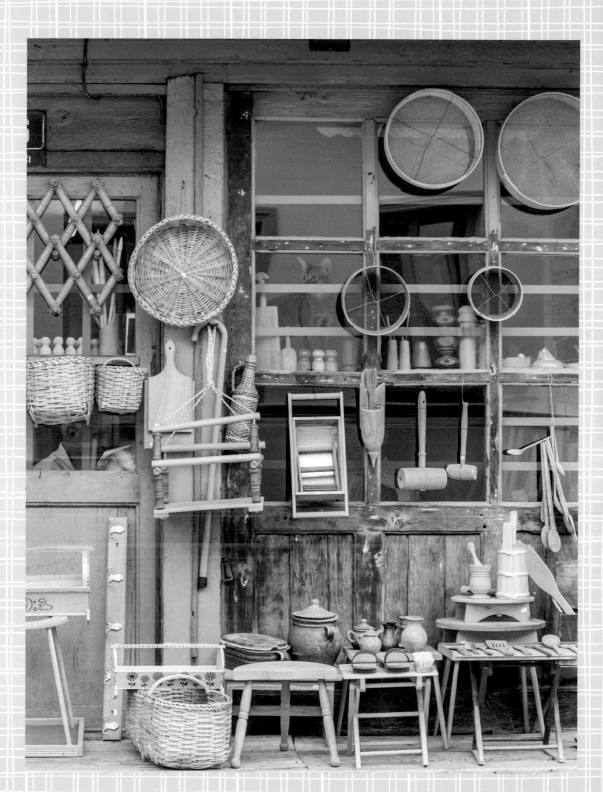

Answer on page 135.

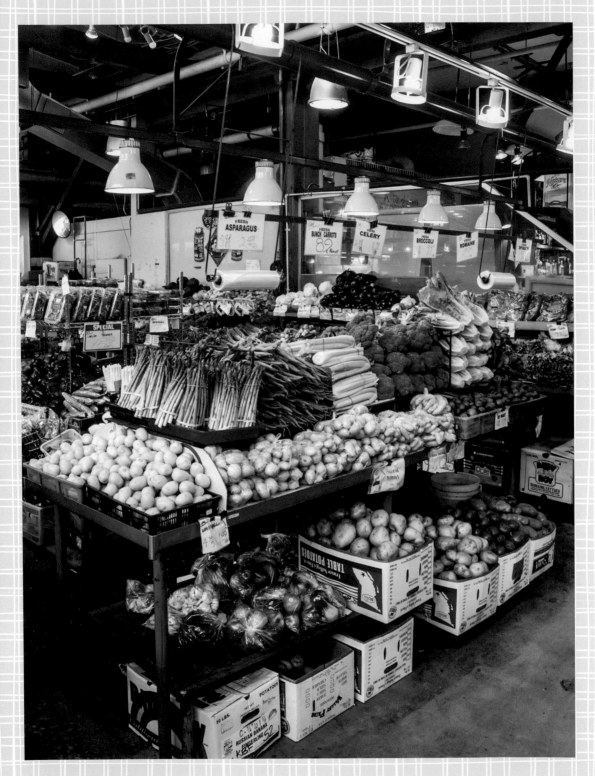

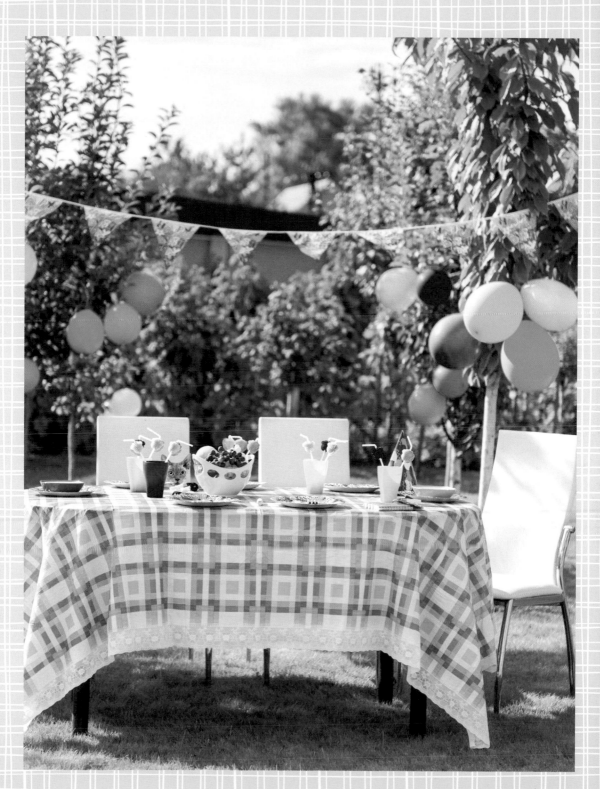

Answer on page 136.

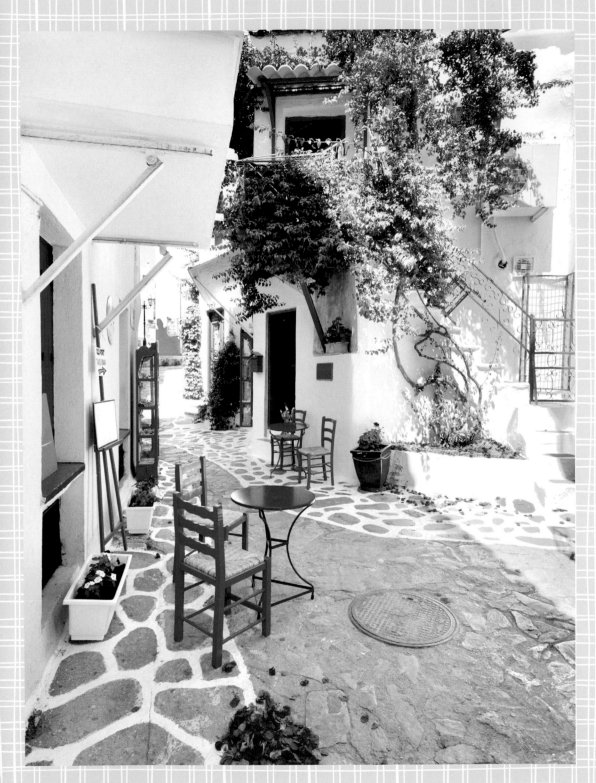

Answer on page 136.

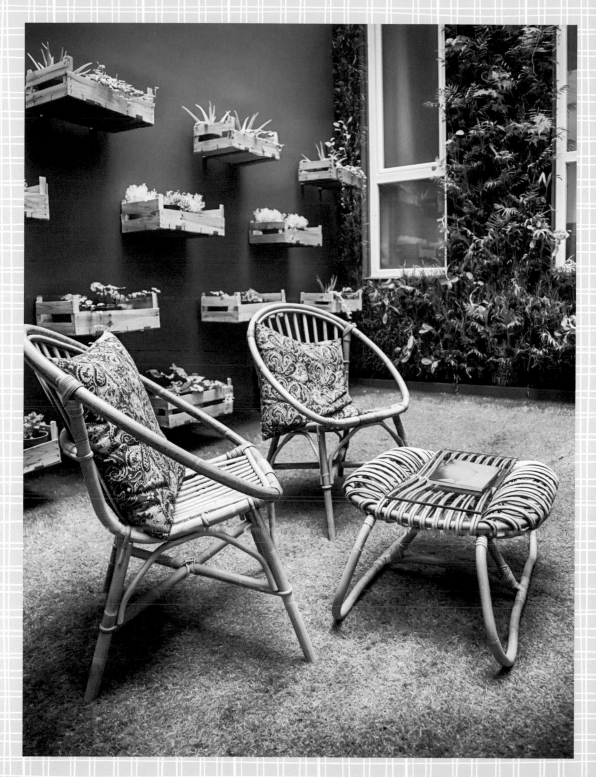

Answer on page 136.

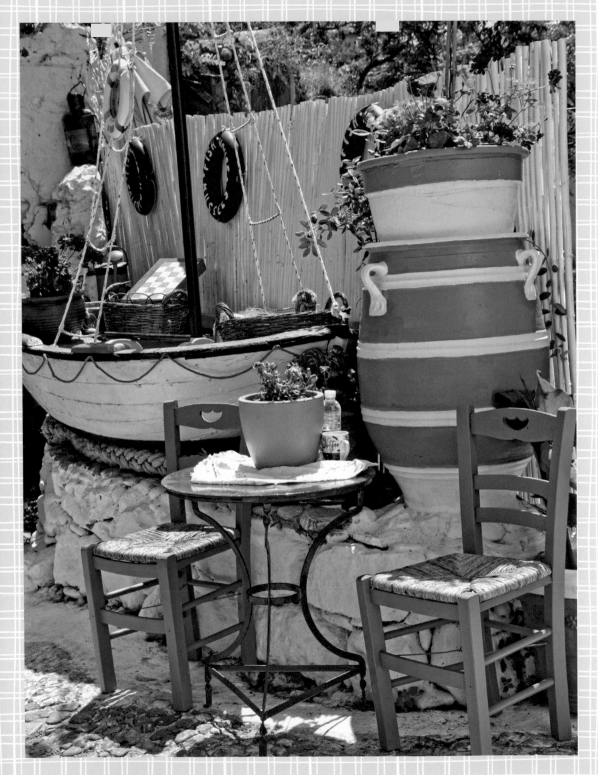

Answer on page 136.

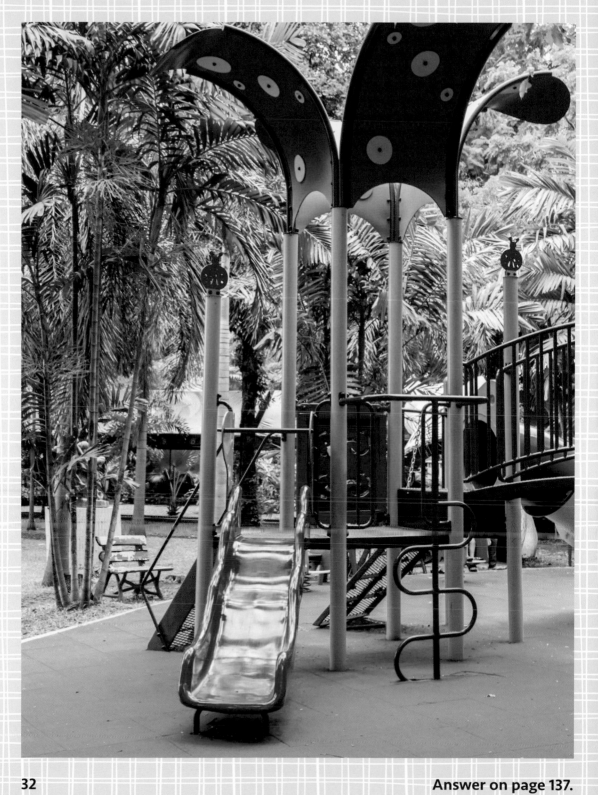

Answer on page 137.

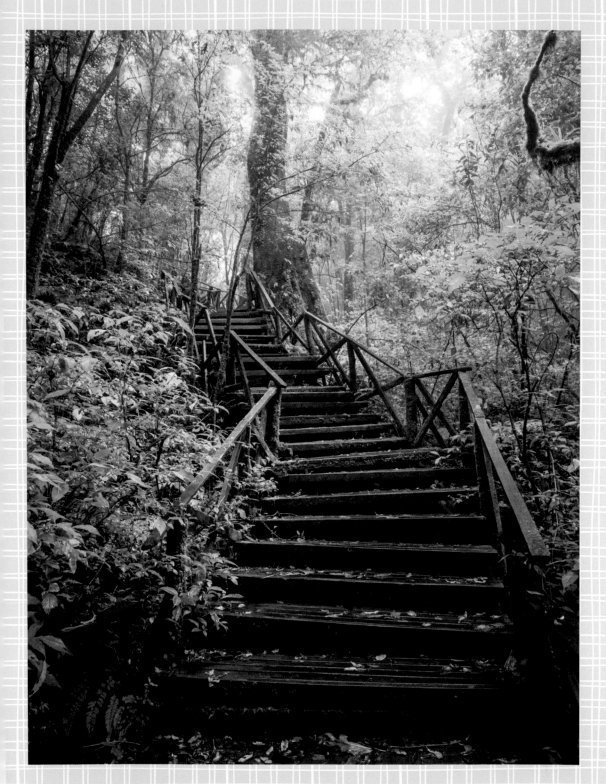

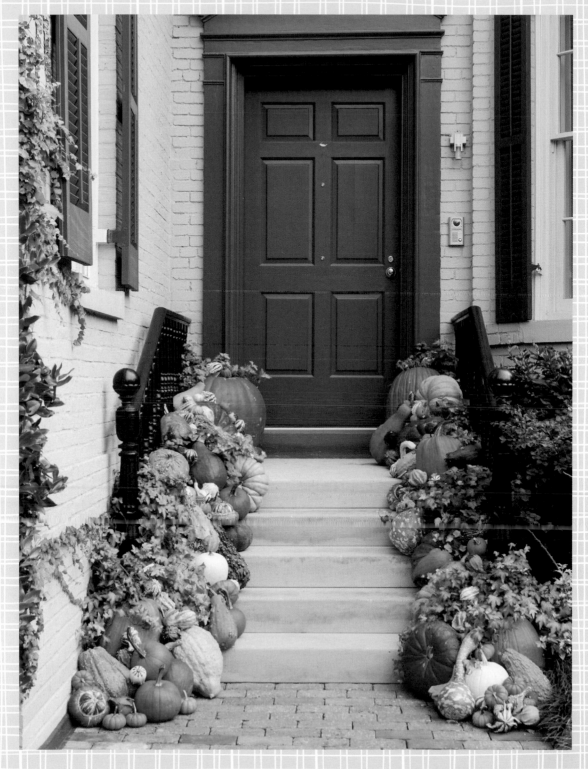

Answer on page 137.

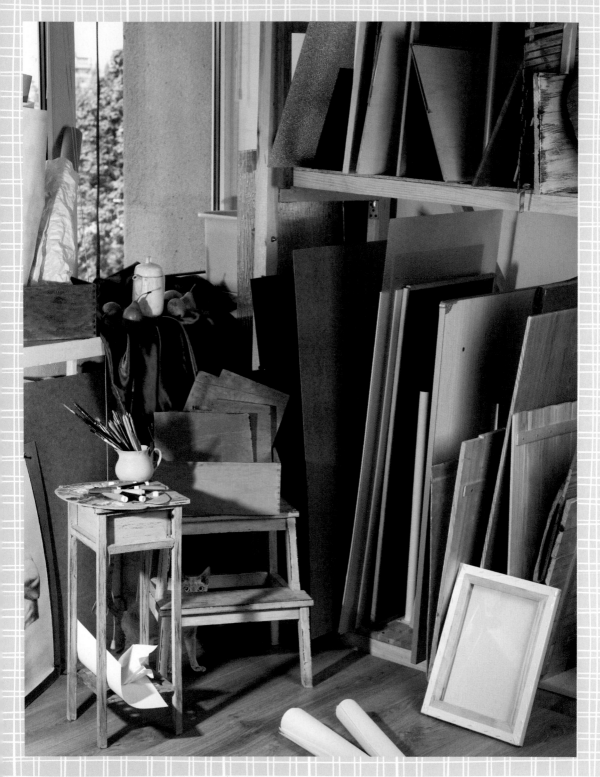

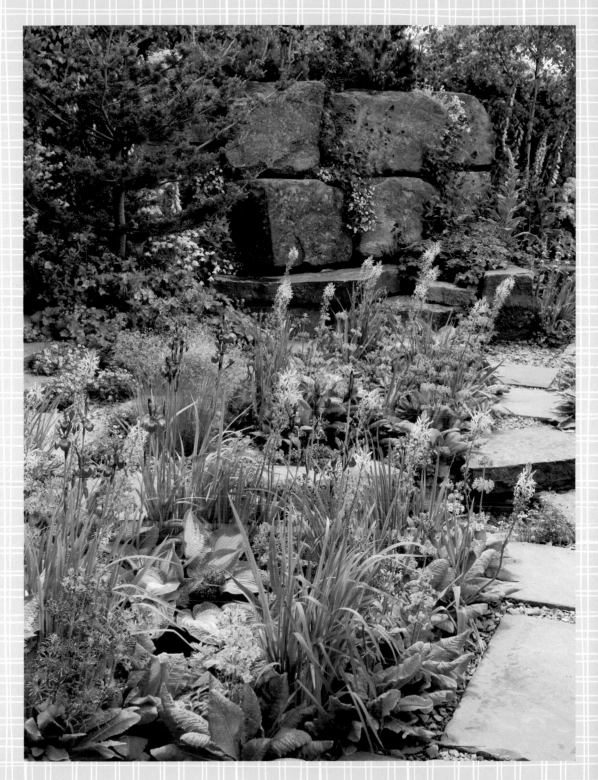

Answer on page 138.

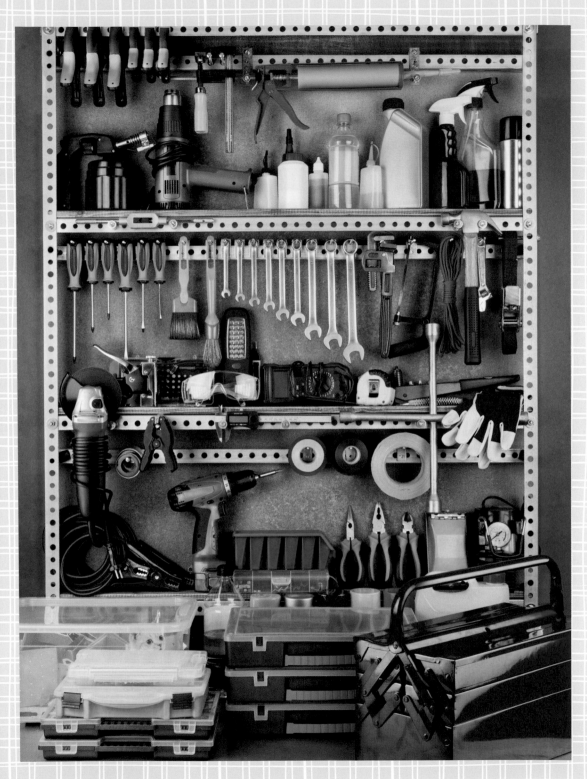

Answer on page 138.

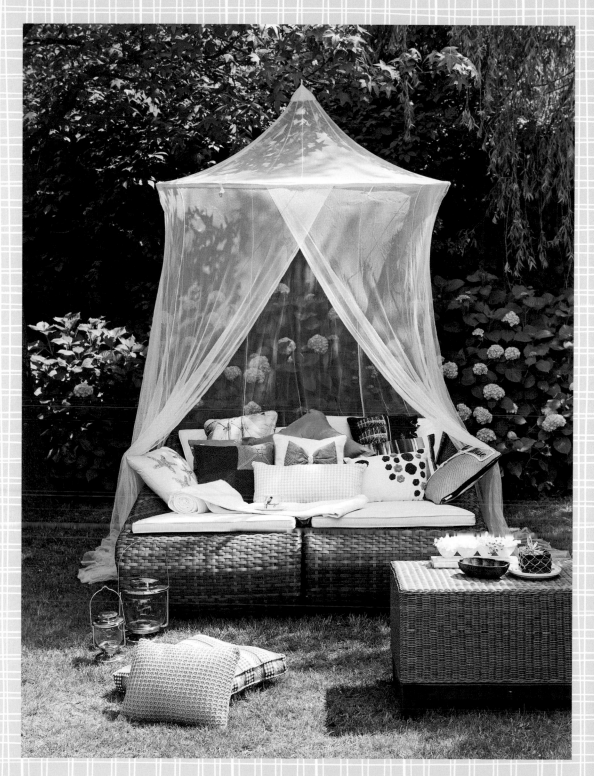

Answer on page 138.

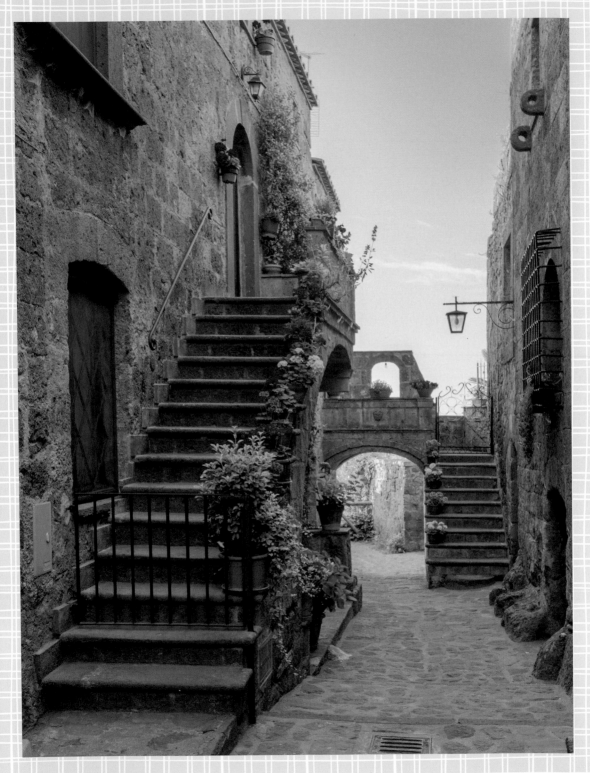

Answer on page 138.

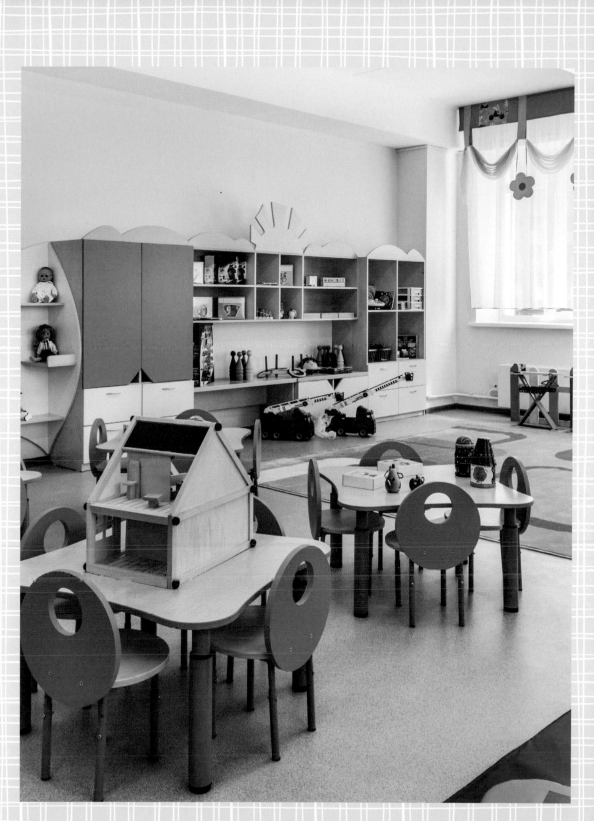

Answer on page 139.

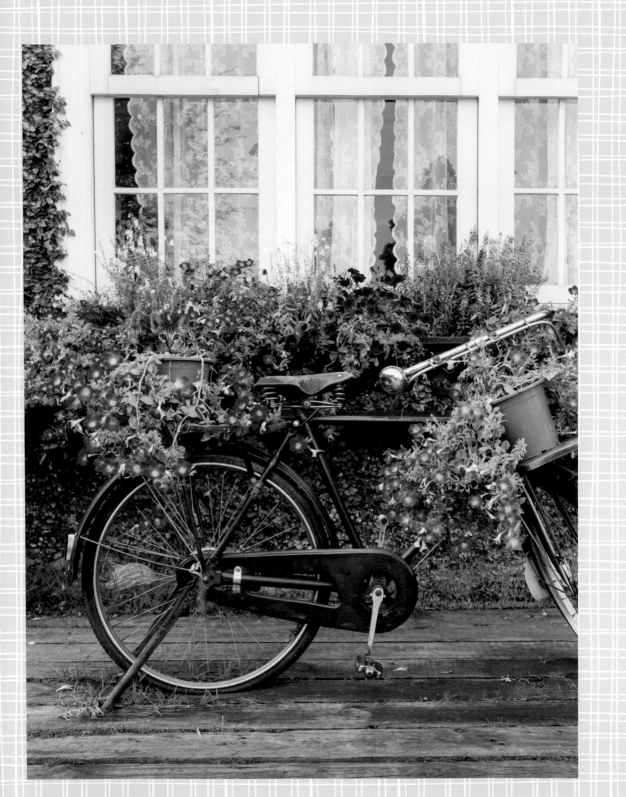

Answer on page 139.

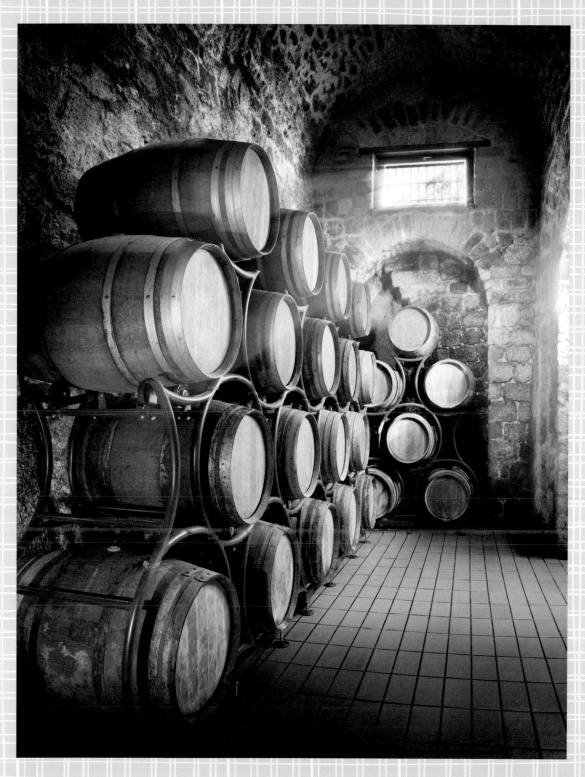

Answer on page 139.

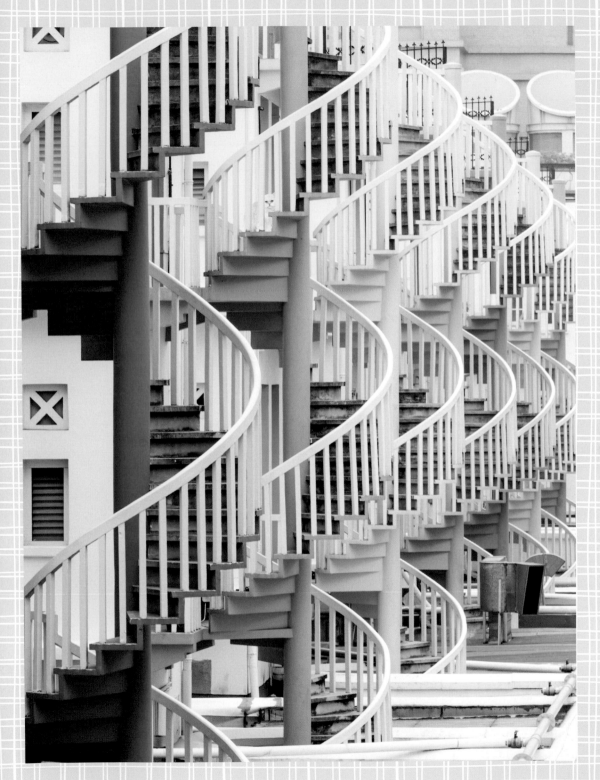

Answer on page 139.

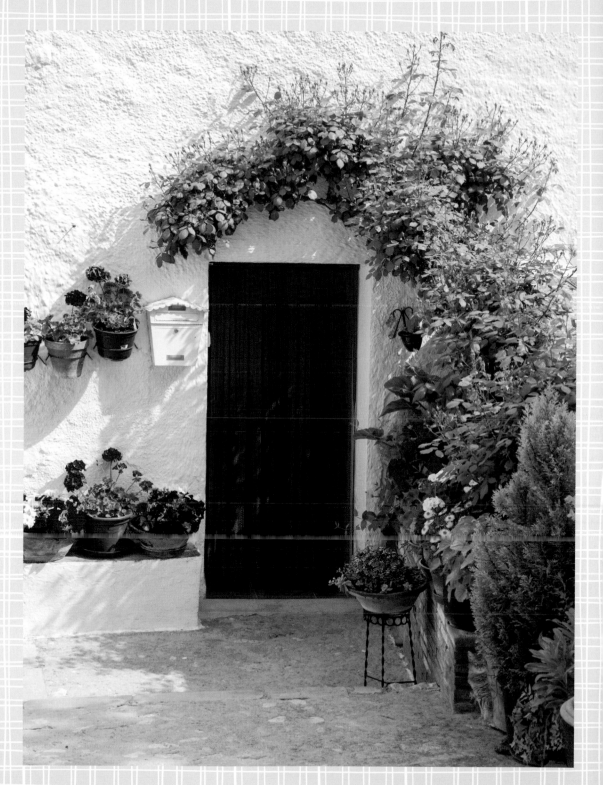

Answer on page 140.

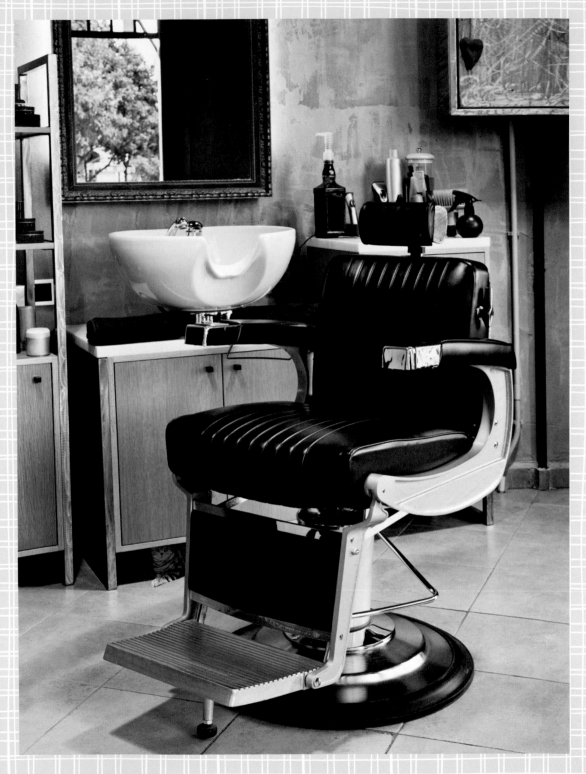

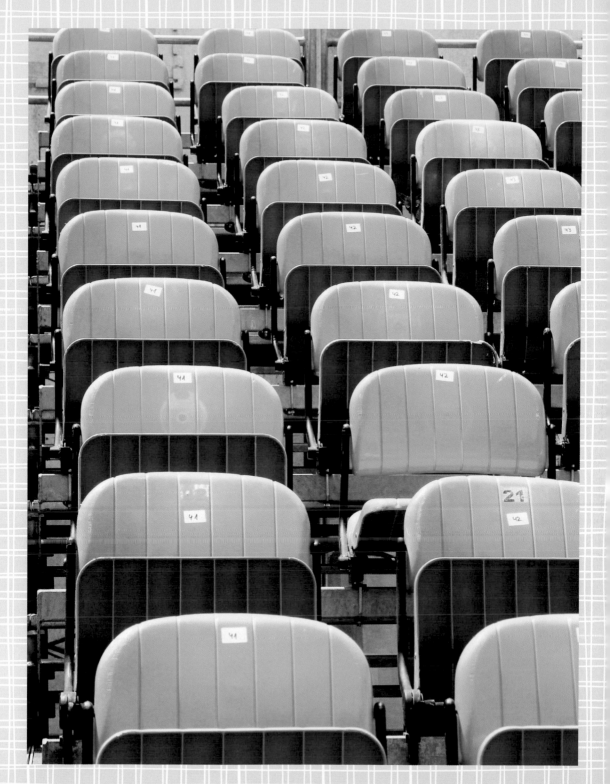

Answer on page 140.

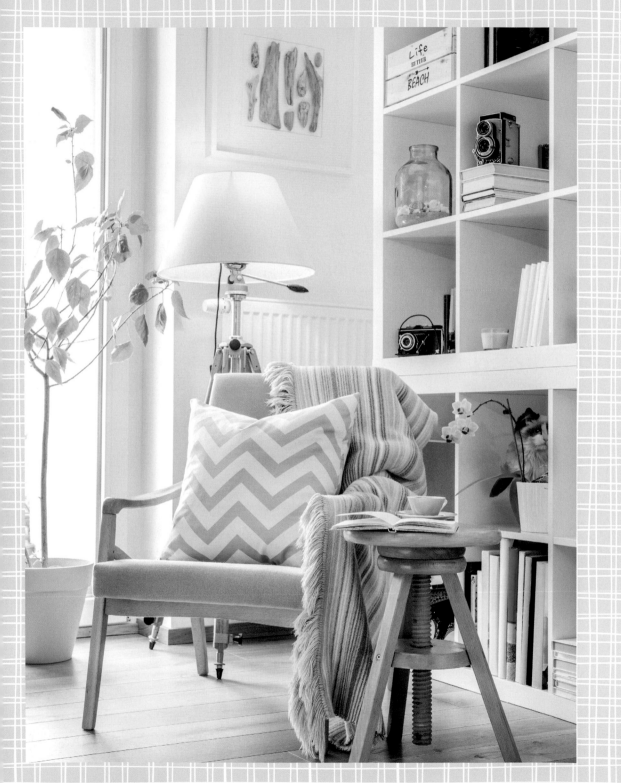

Answer on page 140.

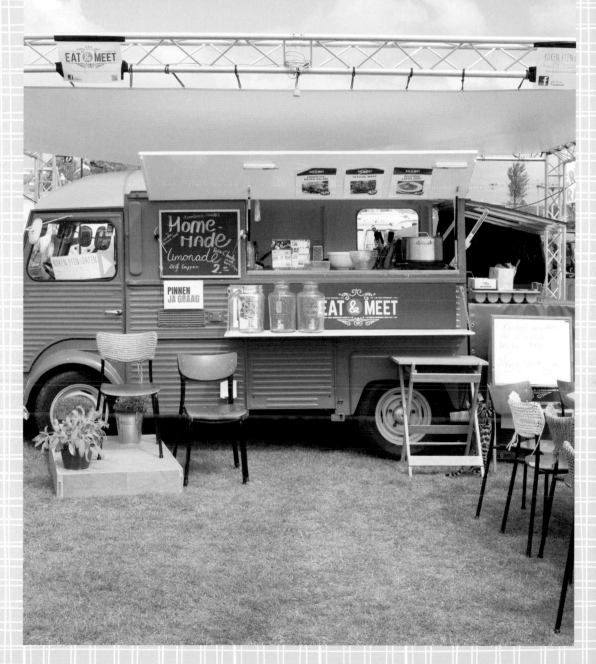

Answer on page 141.

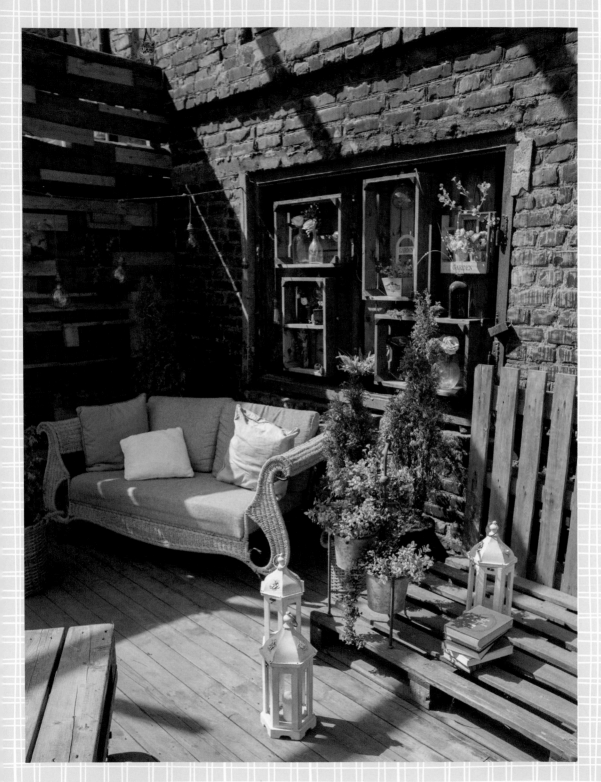

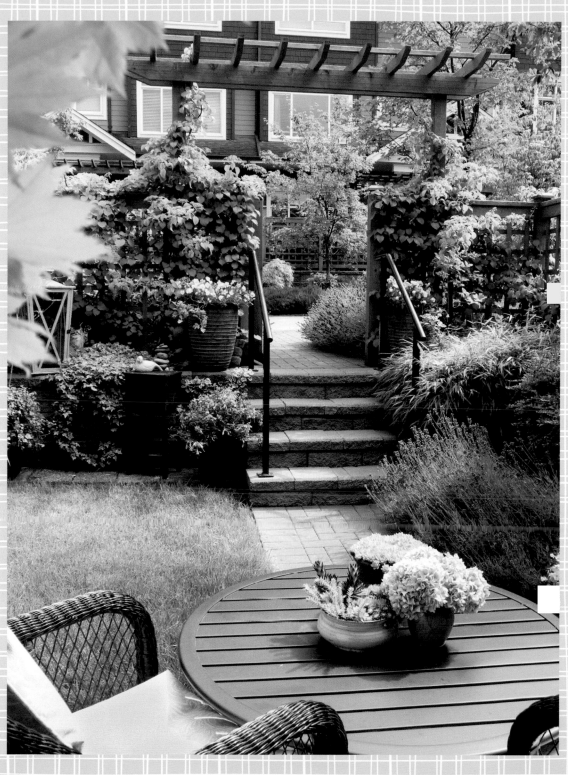

 Answer on page 141.

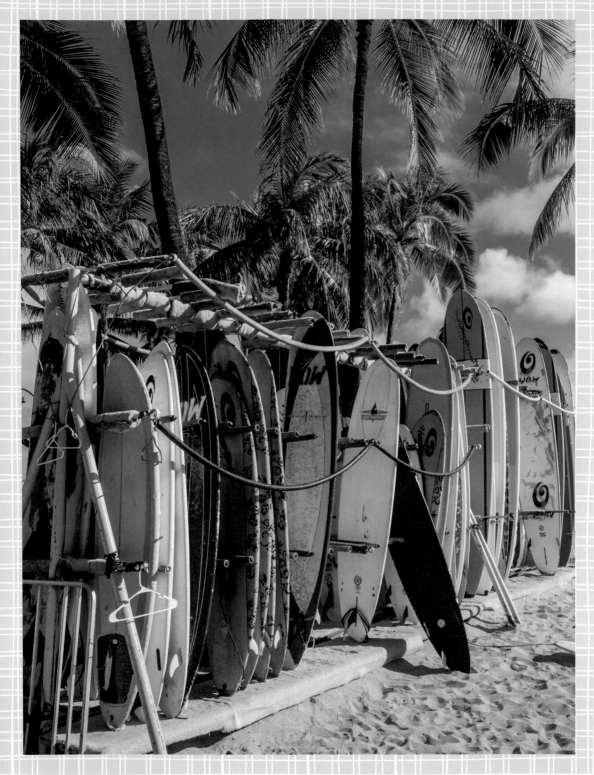

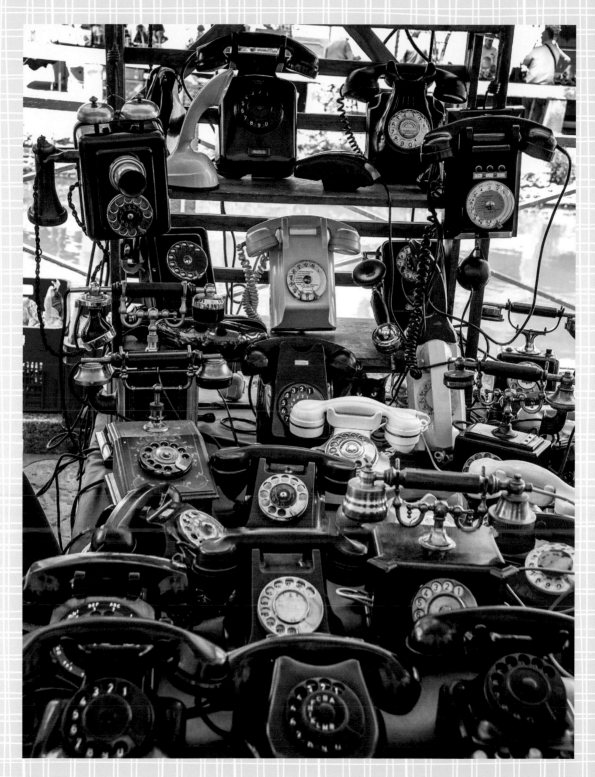

Answer on page 142.

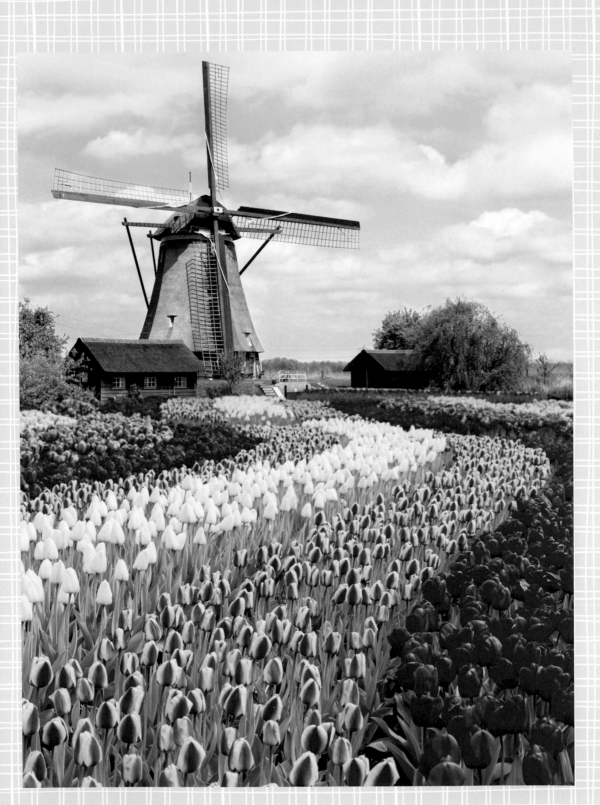

Answer on page 142.

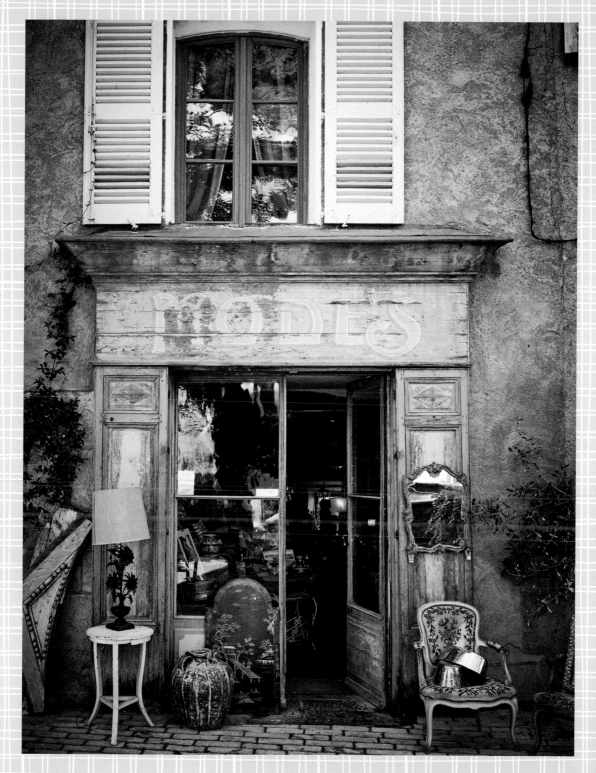

Answer on page 142.

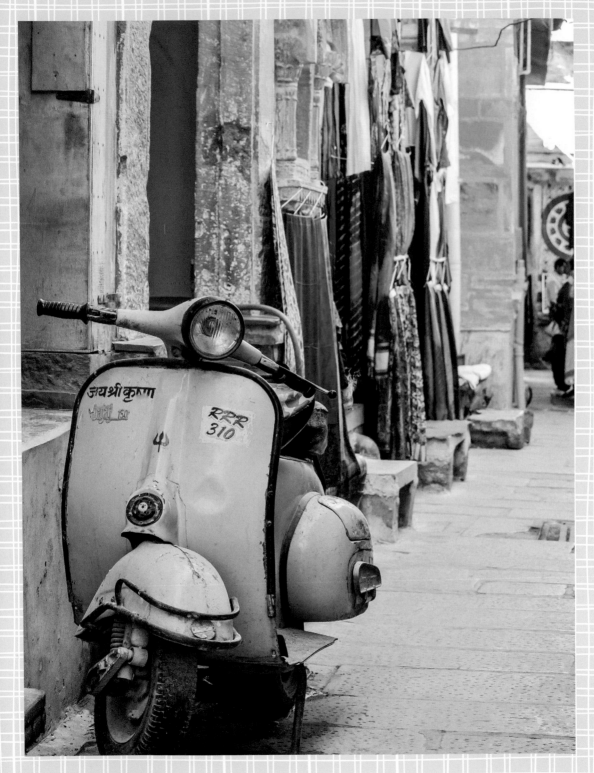

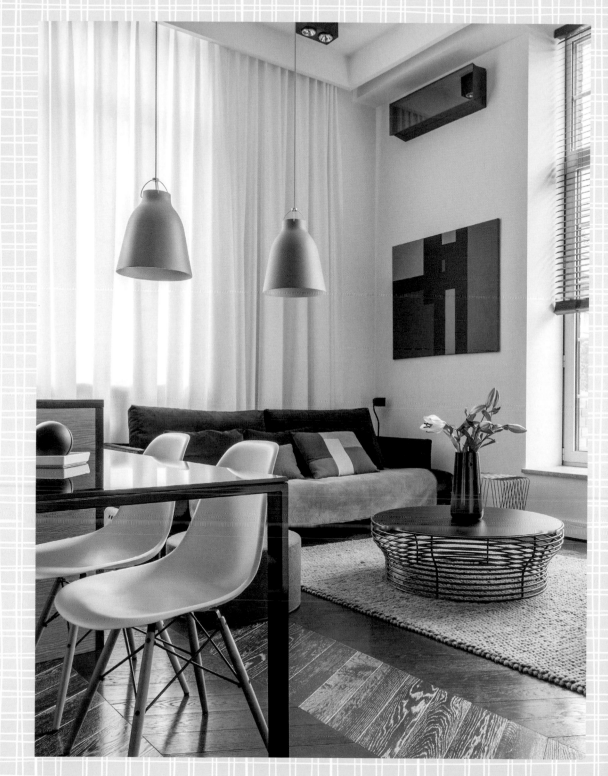

Answer on page 143.

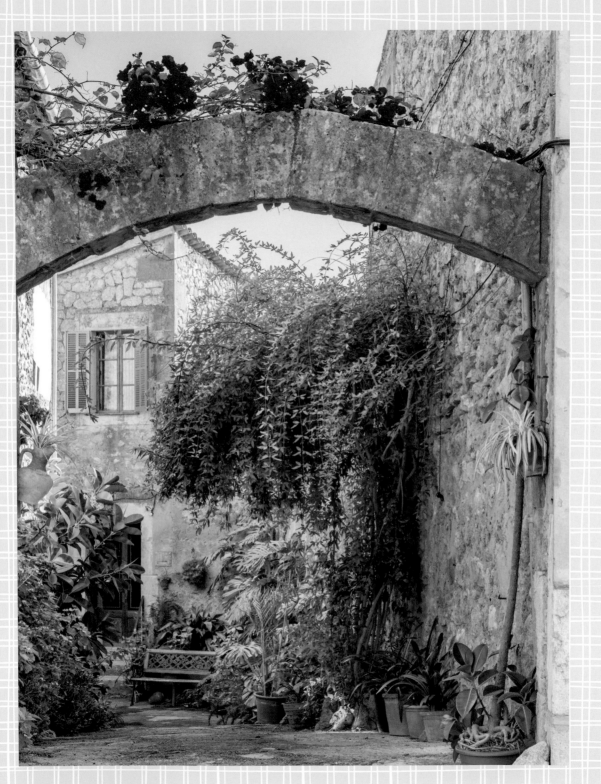

Answer on page 143.

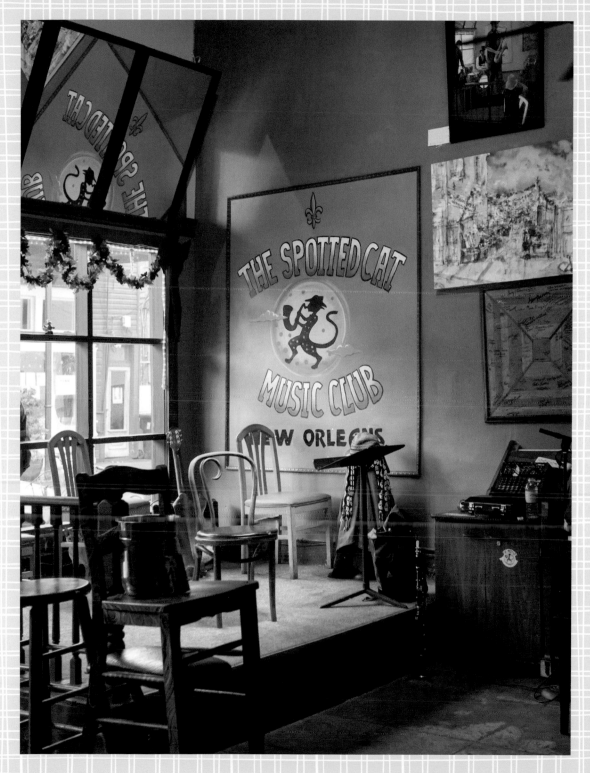

Answer on page 143.

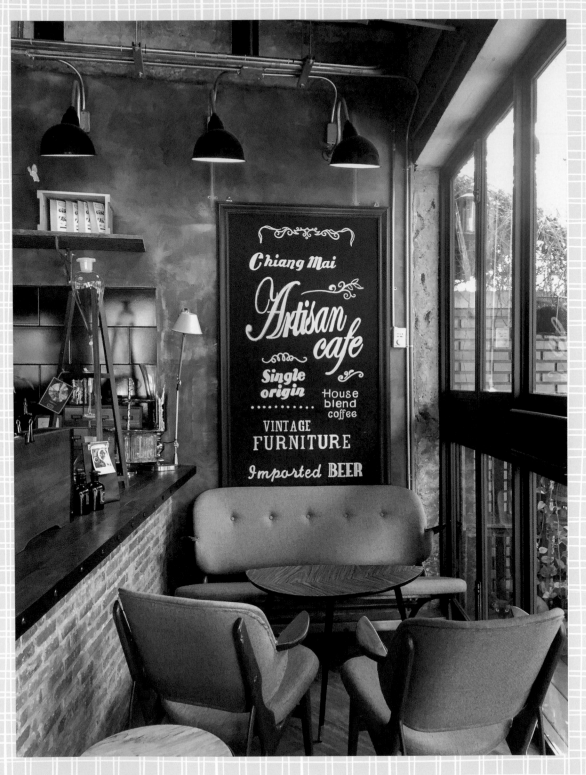

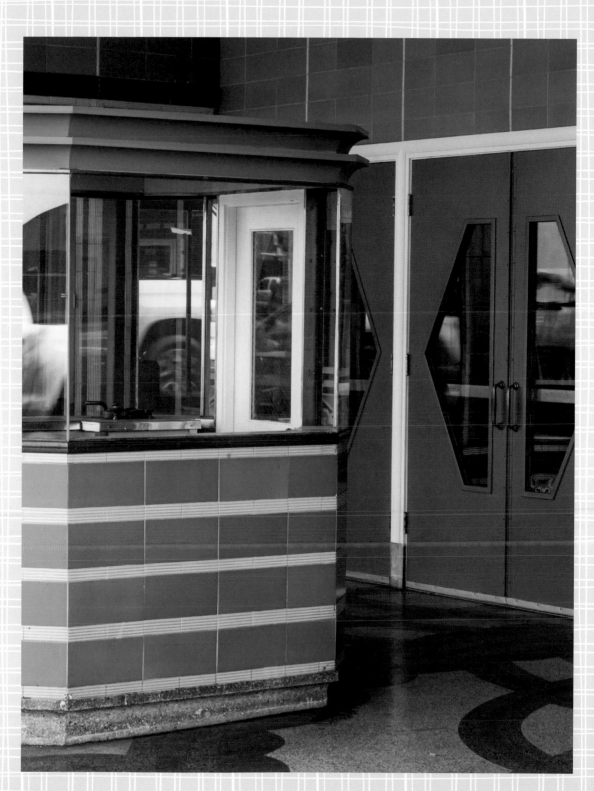

Answer on page 144.

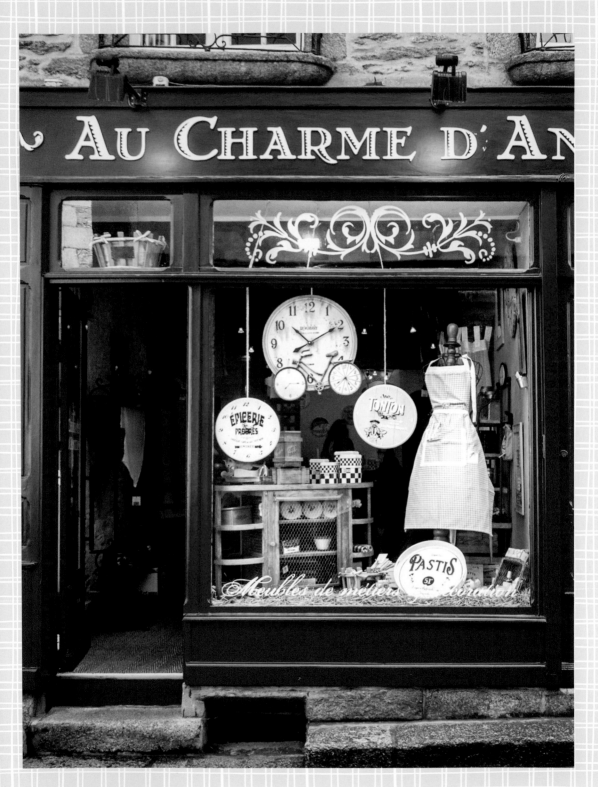

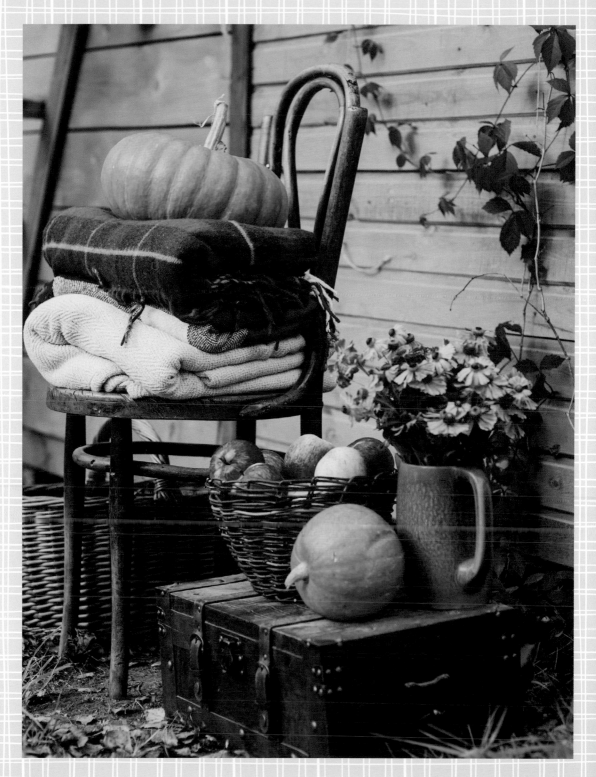

Answer on page 144.

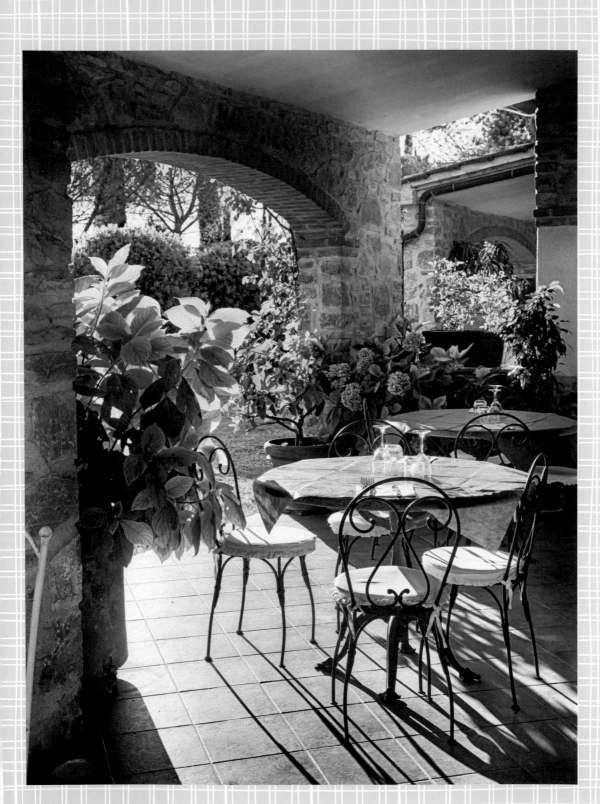

Answer on page 144.

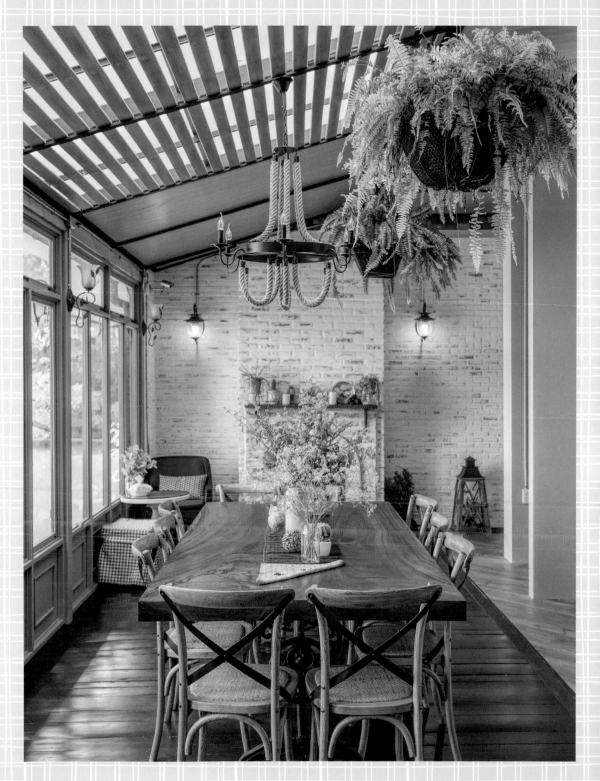

Answer on page 145.

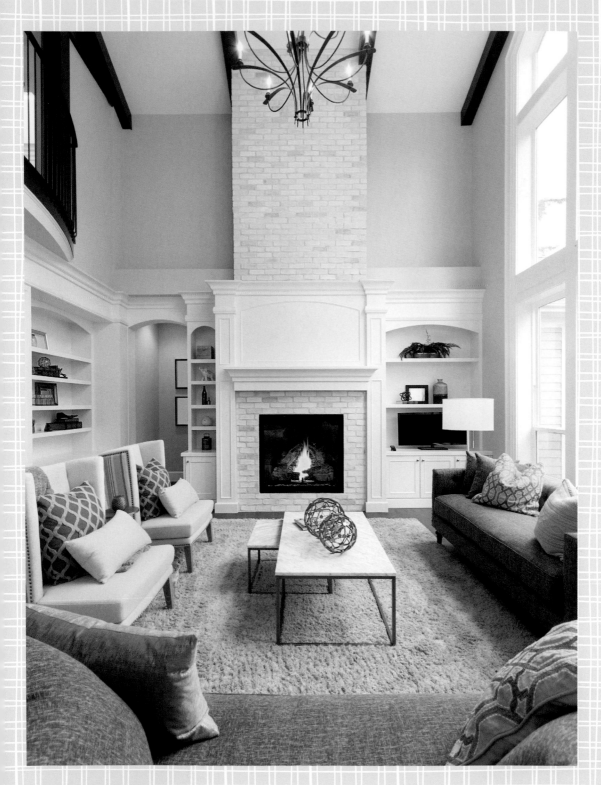

Answer on page 145.

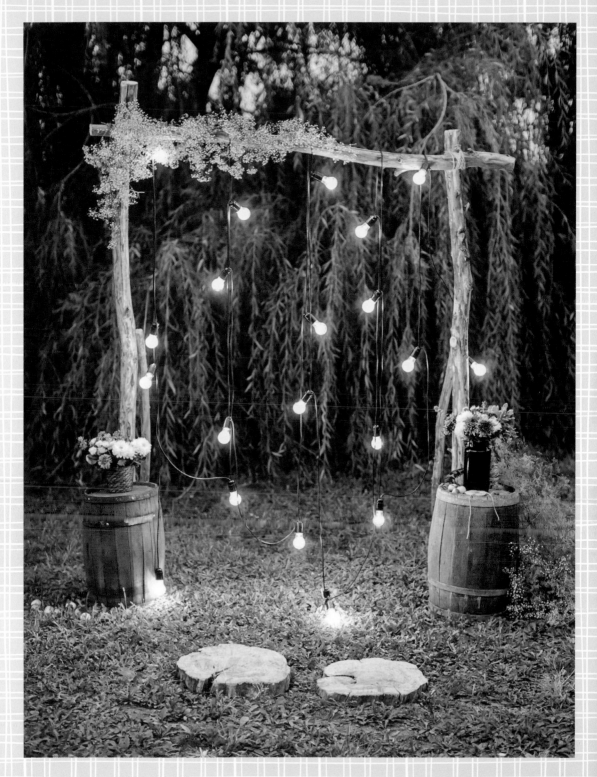

Answer on page 145.

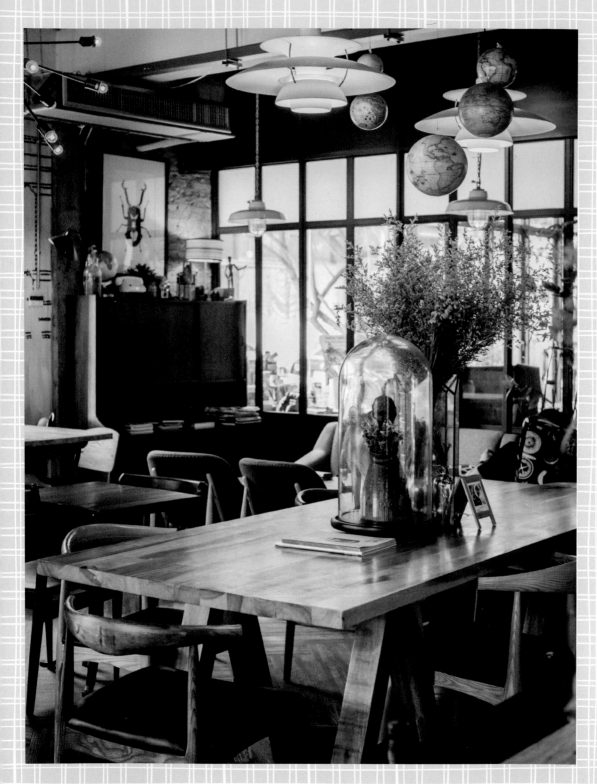

Answer on page 145.

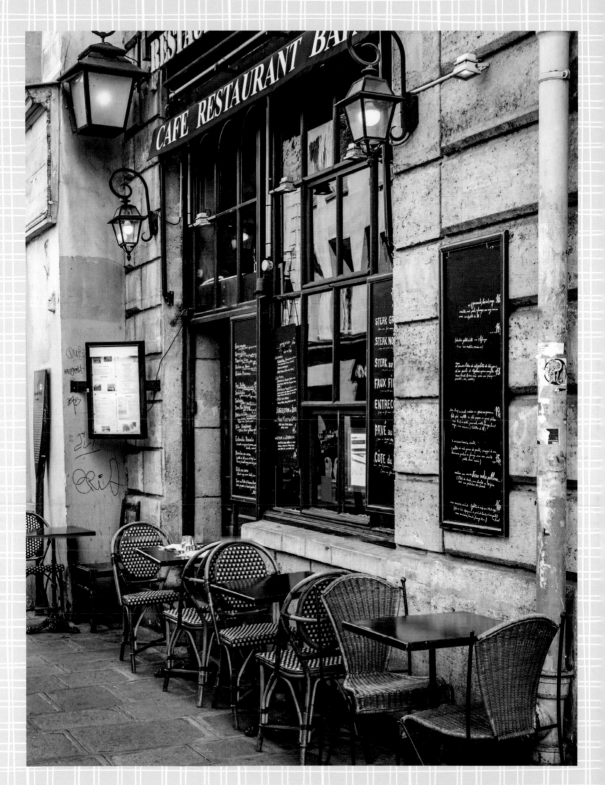

Answer on page 146.

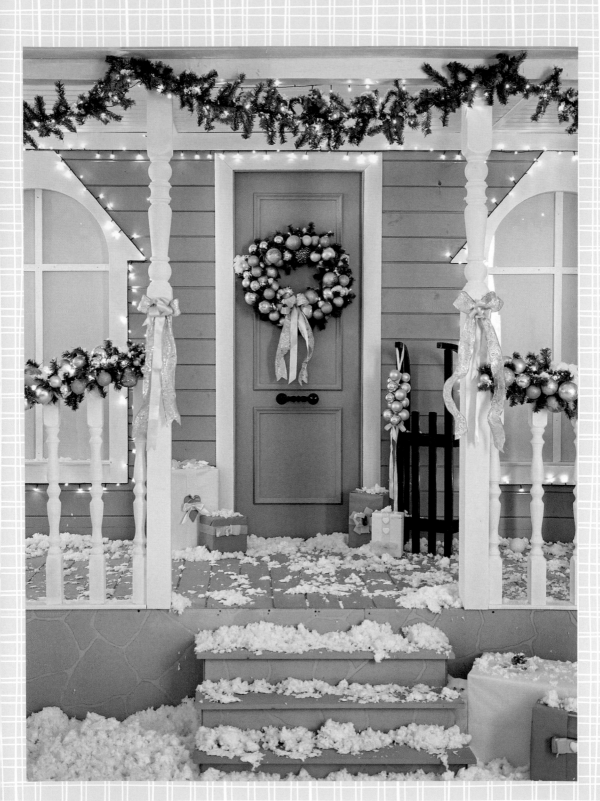

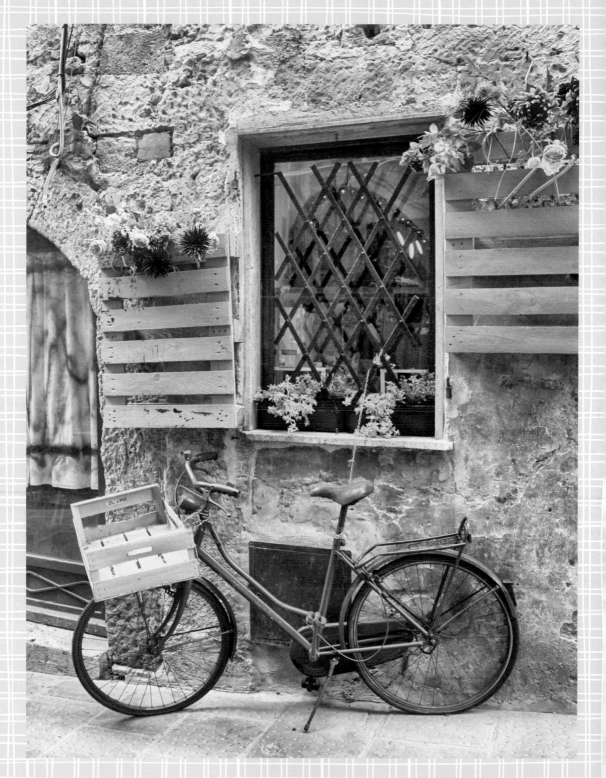

Answer on page 146.

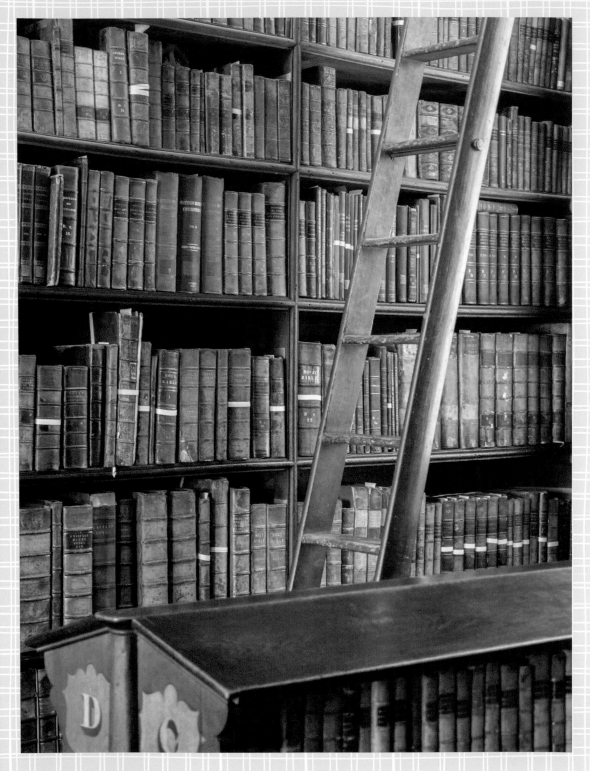

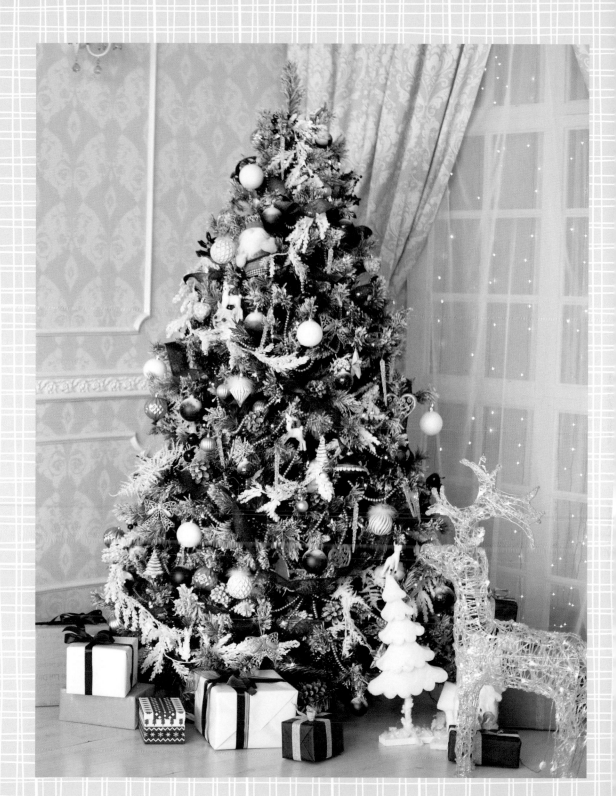

Answer on page 147.

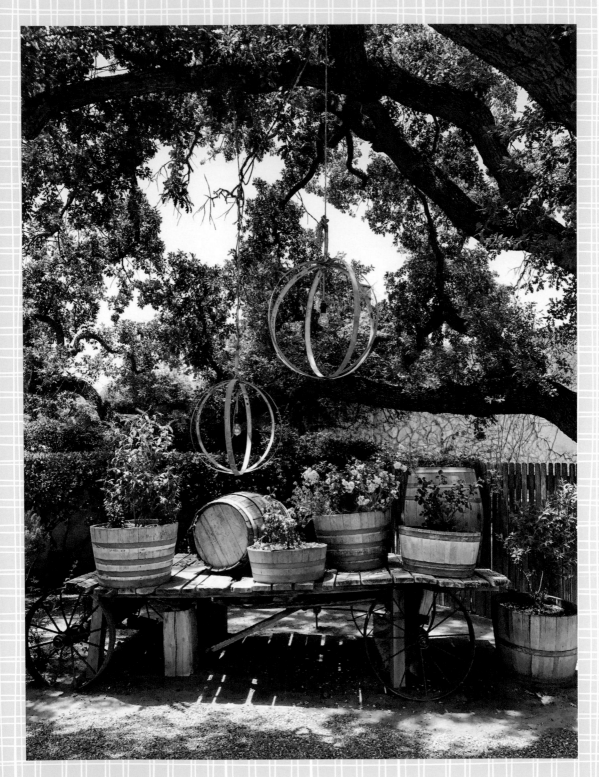

Answer on page 147.

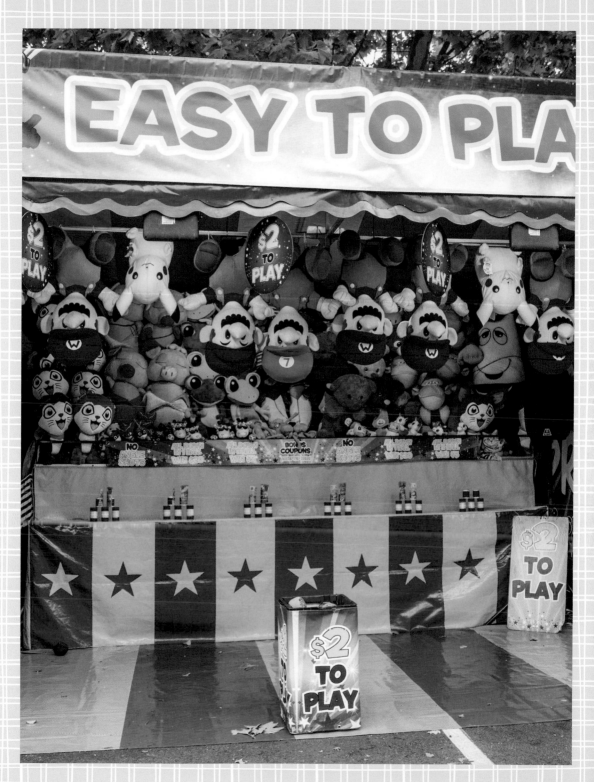

Answer on page 147.

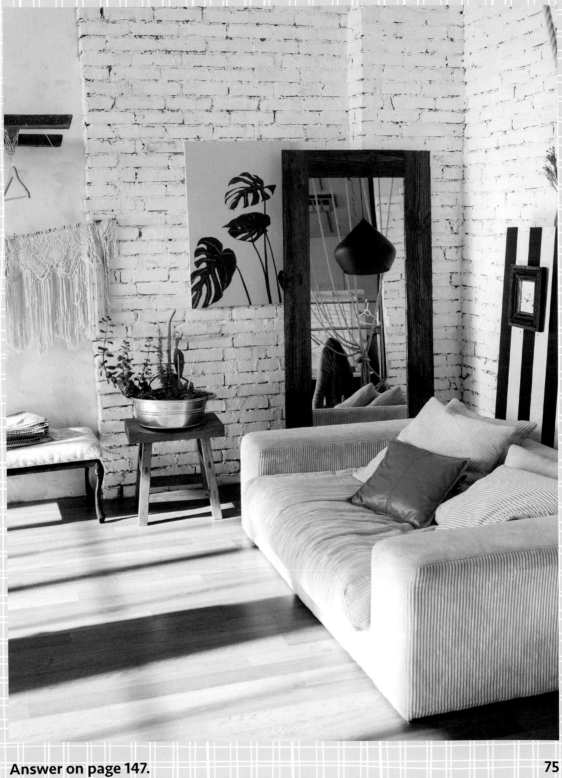

Answer on page 147.

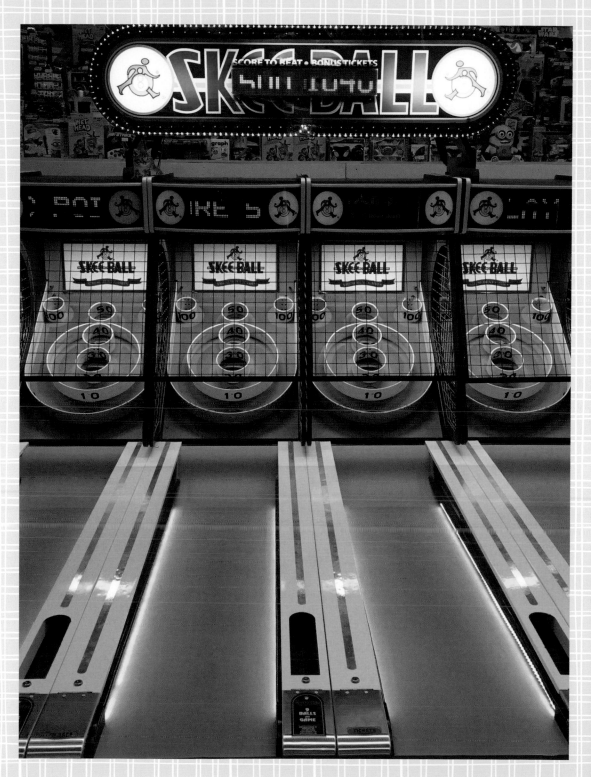

Answer on page 148.

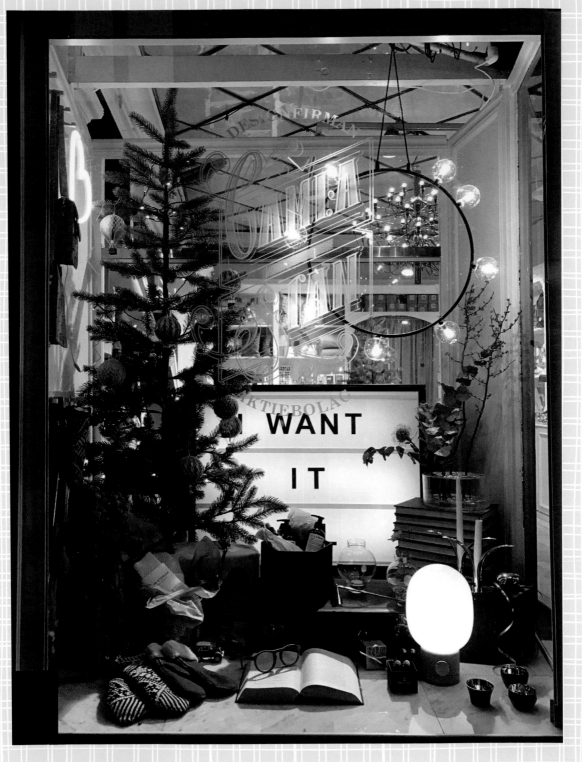

Answer on page 148.

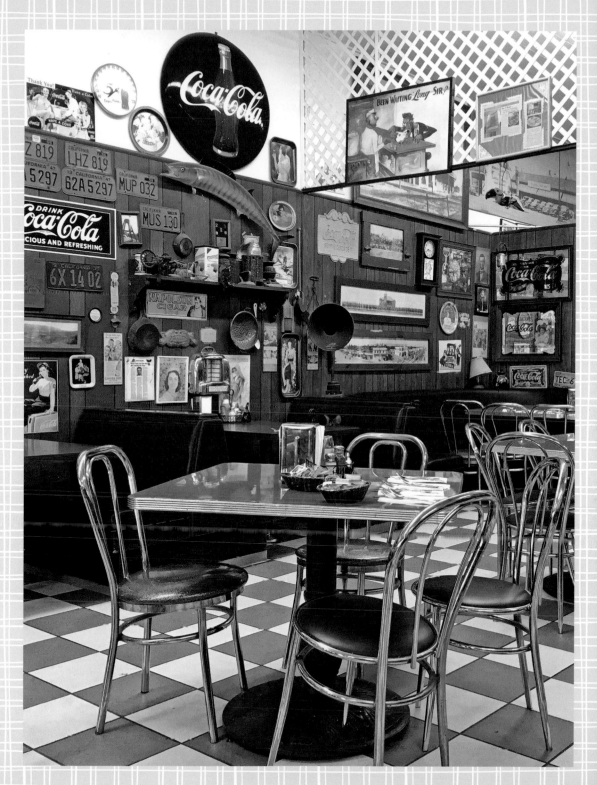

Answer on page 148.

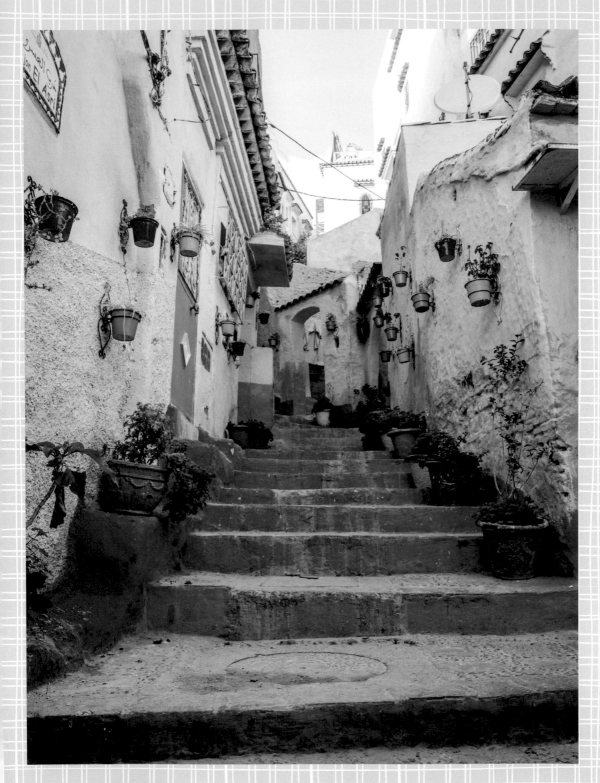

Answer on page 148.

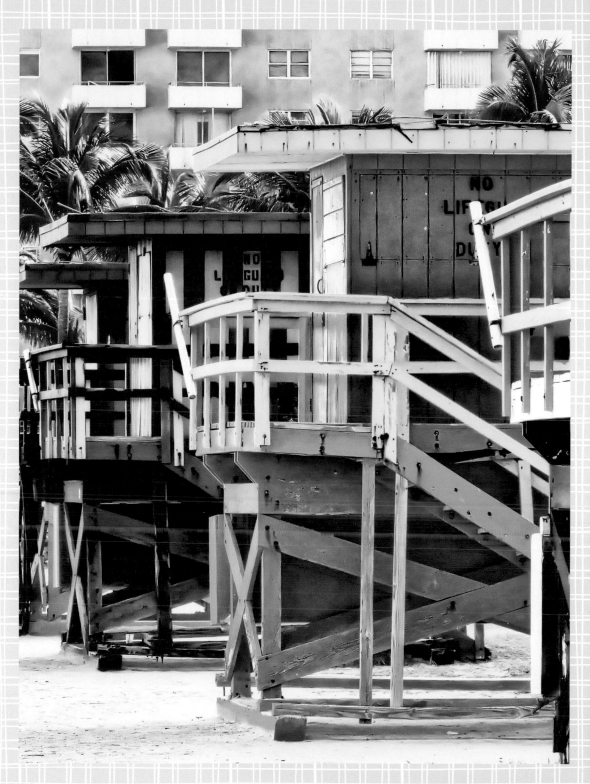

Answer on page 149.

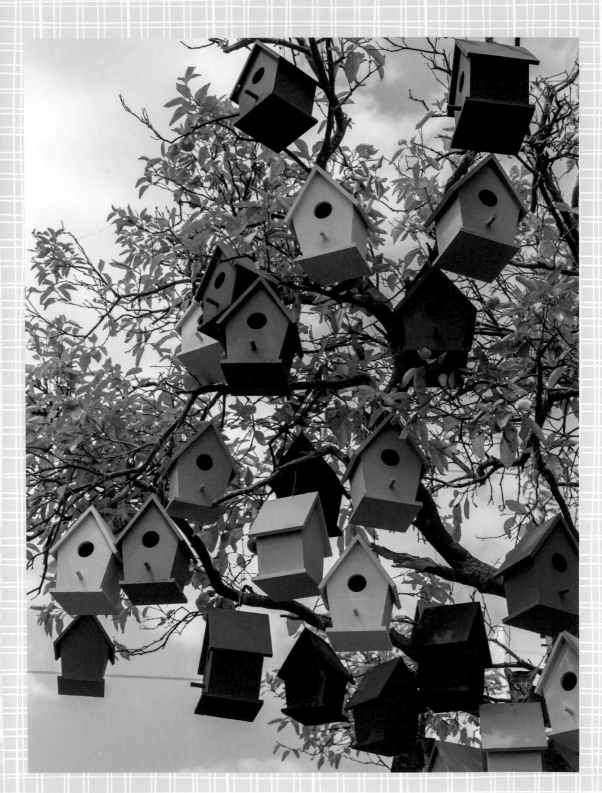

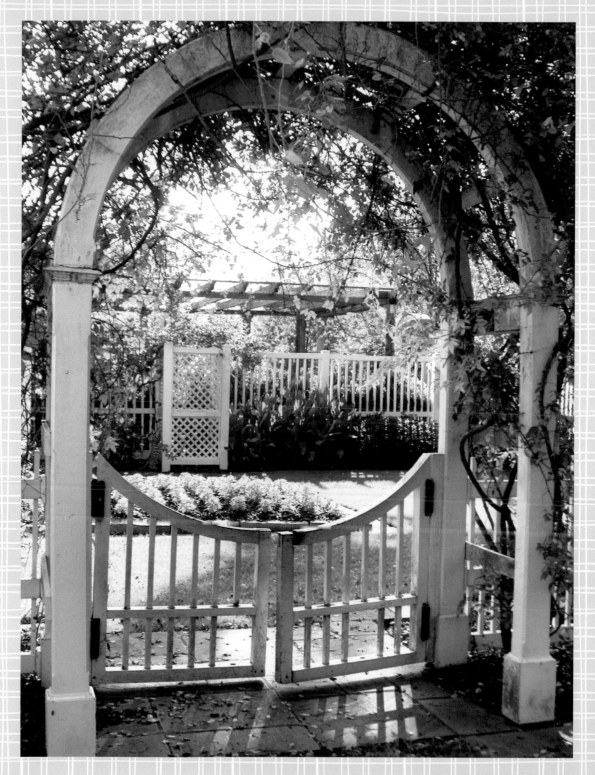

Answer on page 149.

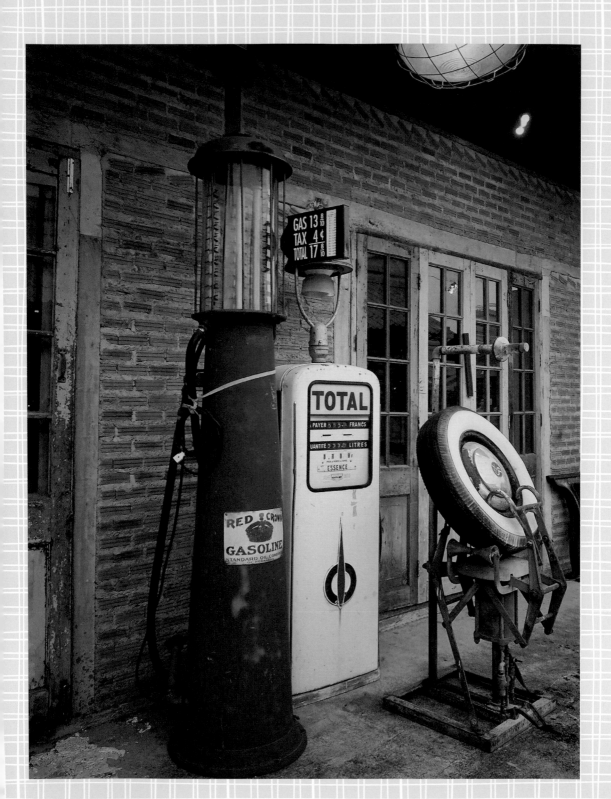

Answer on page 149.

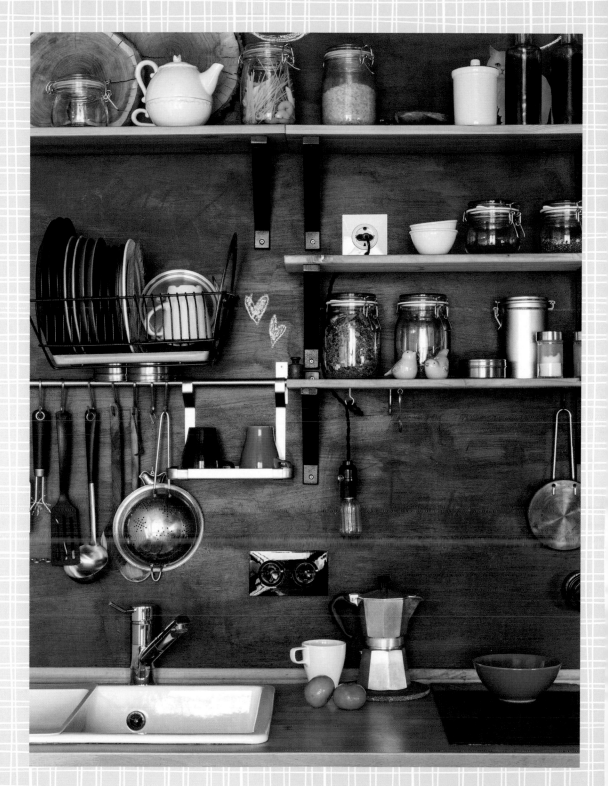

Answer on page 150.

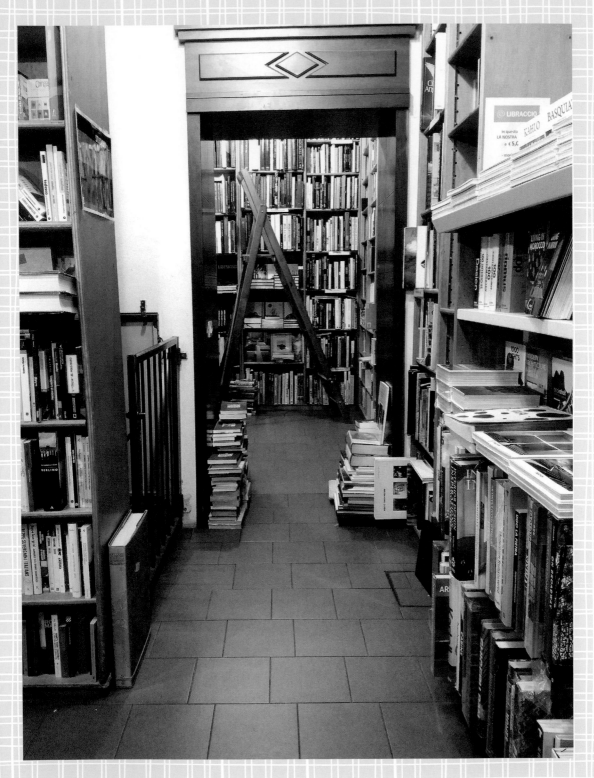

Answer on page 150.

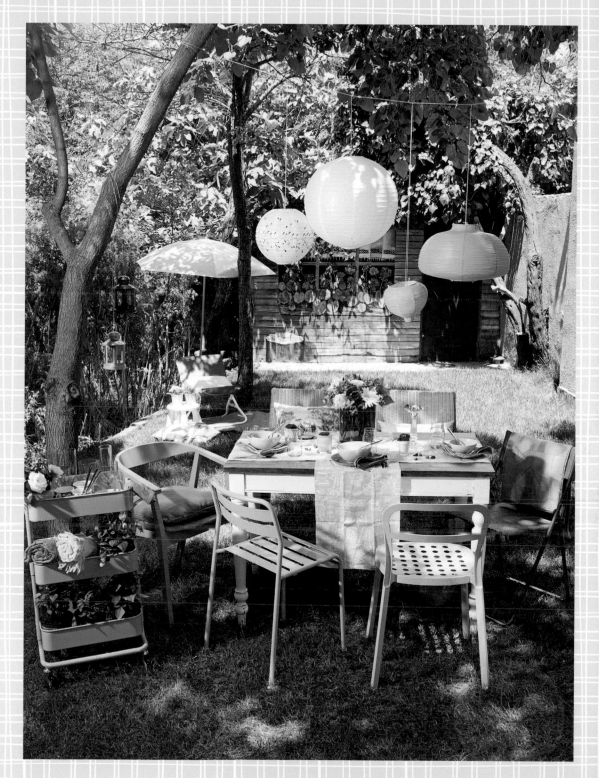

Answer on page 150.

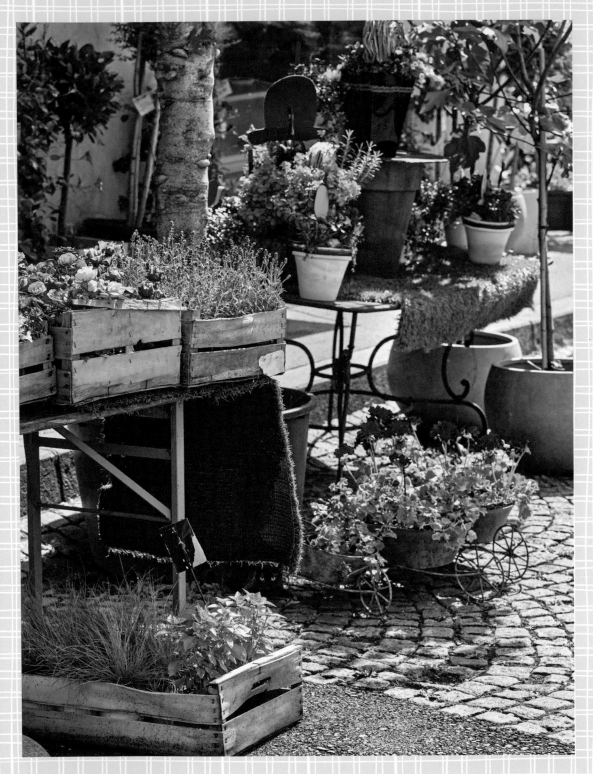

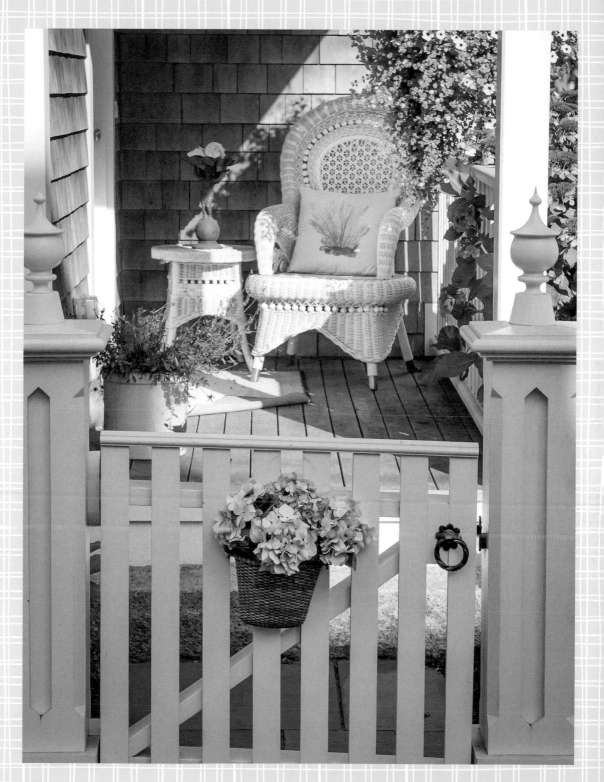

Answer on page 151.

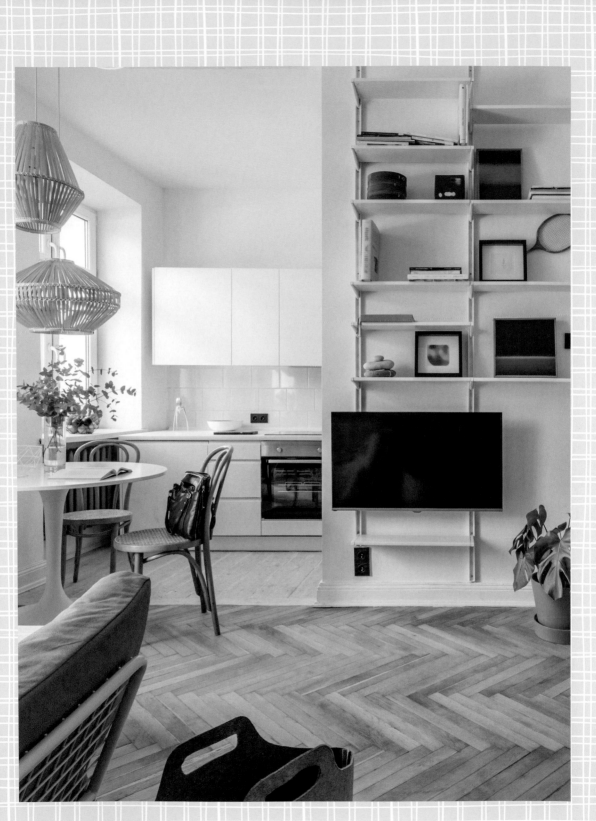

Answer on page 151.

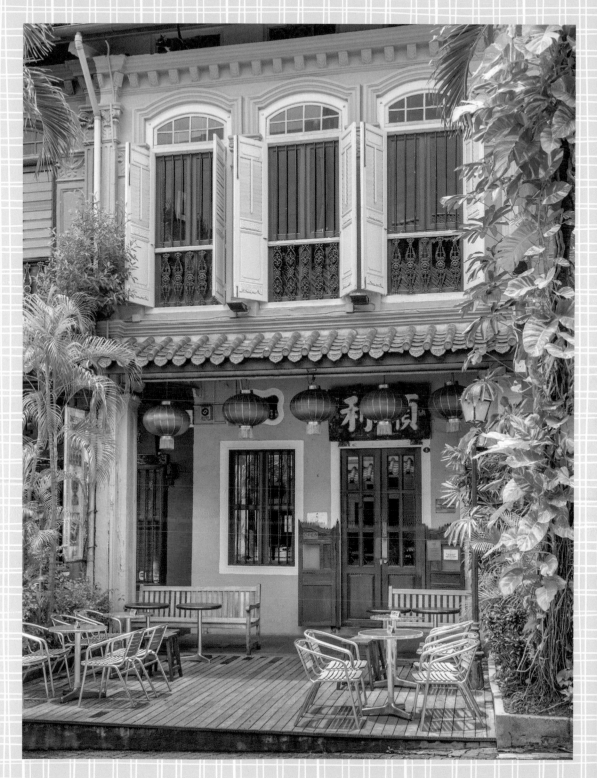

Answer on page 151.

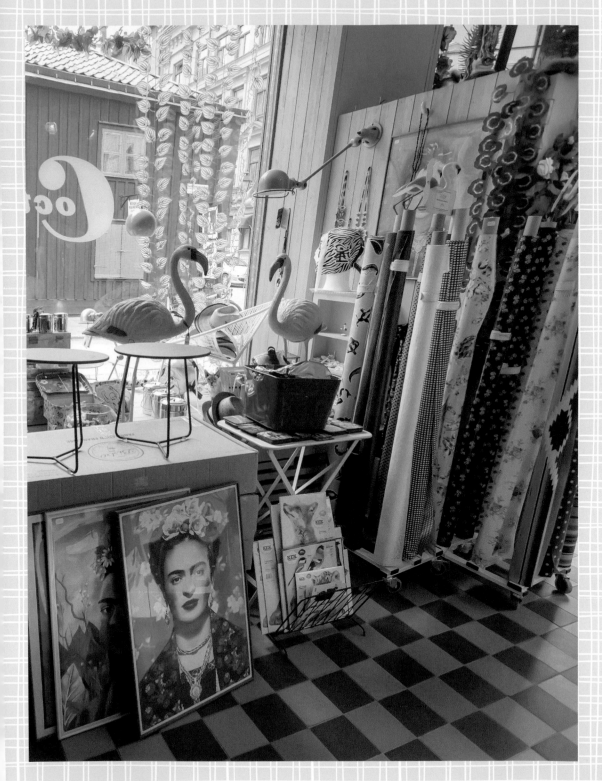

Answer on page 151.

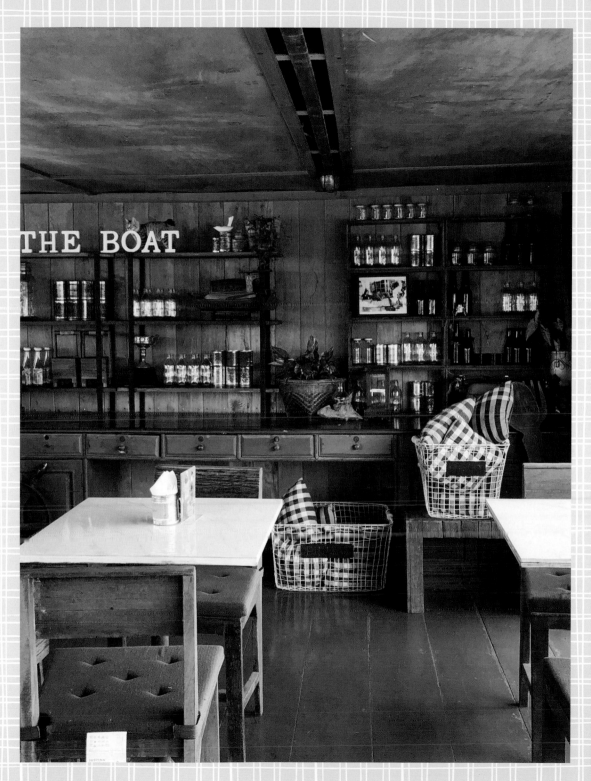

Answer on page 152.

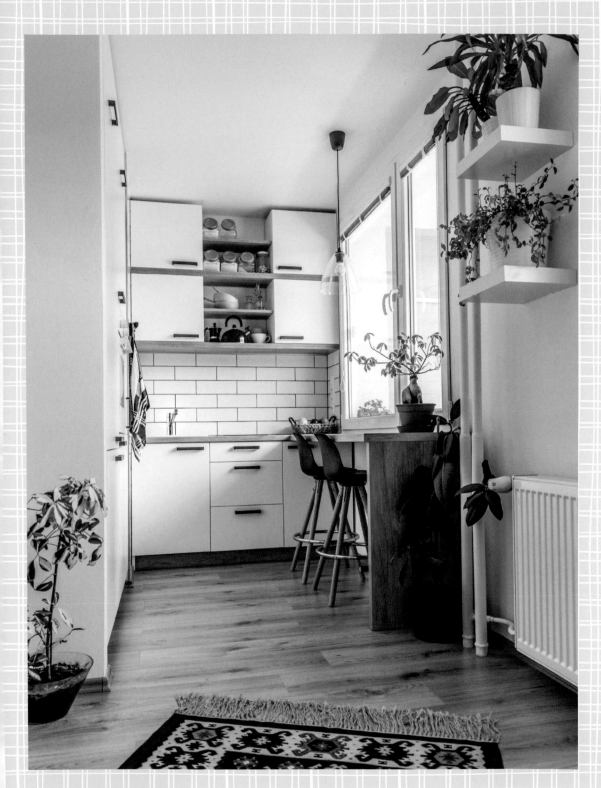

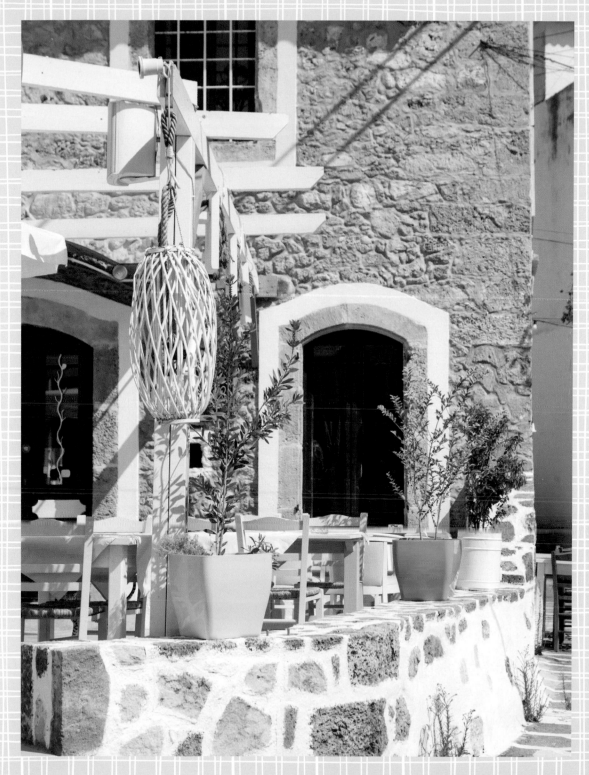

Answer on page 152.

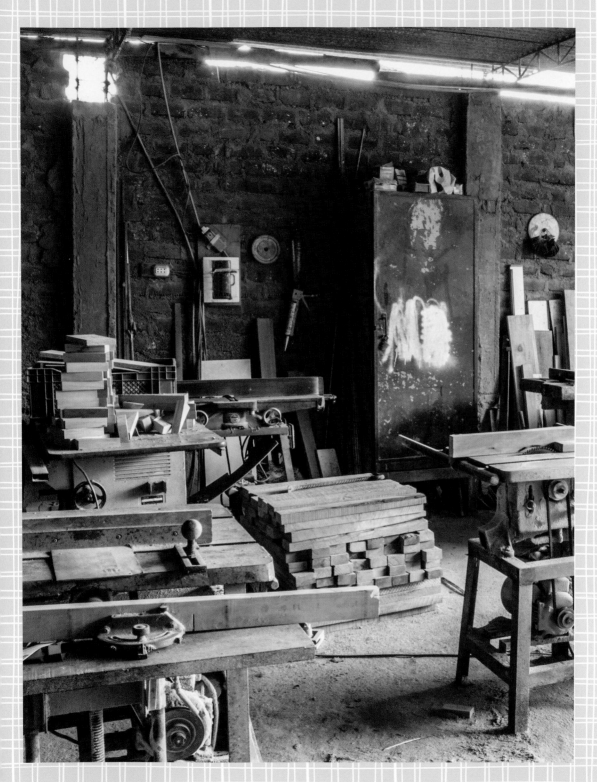

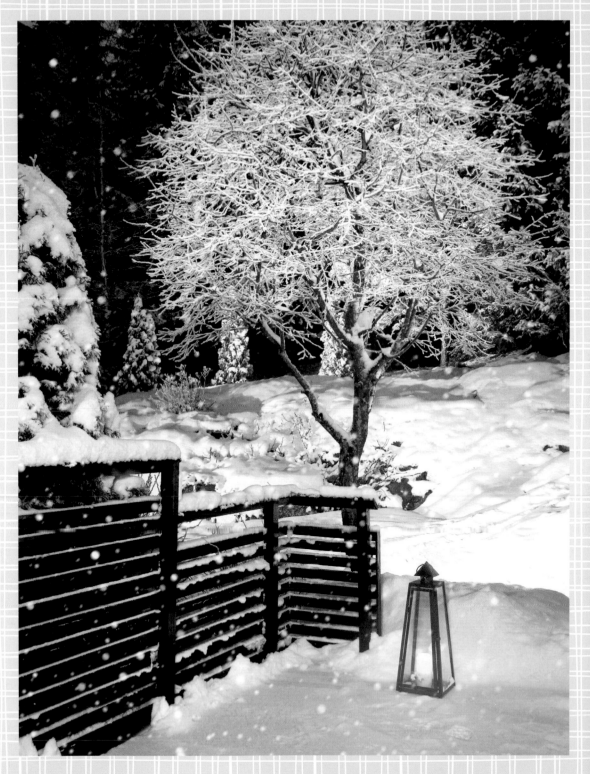

Answer on page 153.

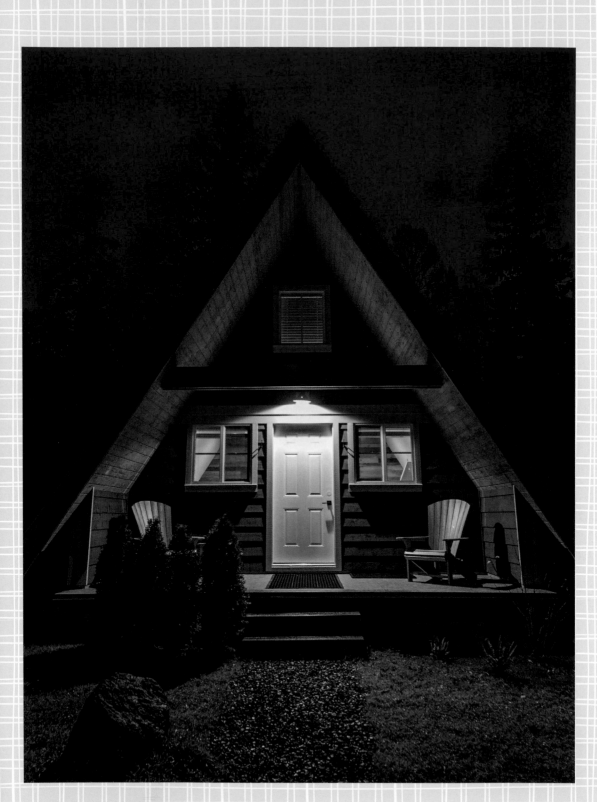

Answer on page 153.

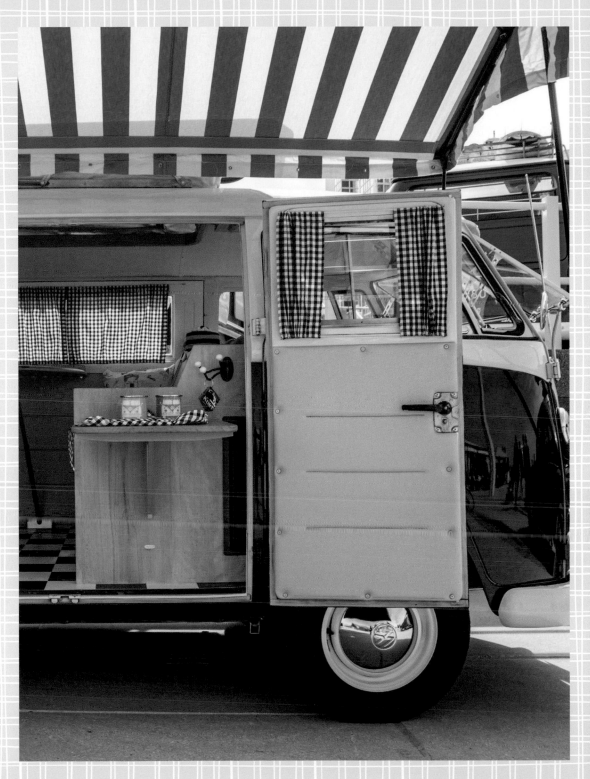

Answer on page 153.

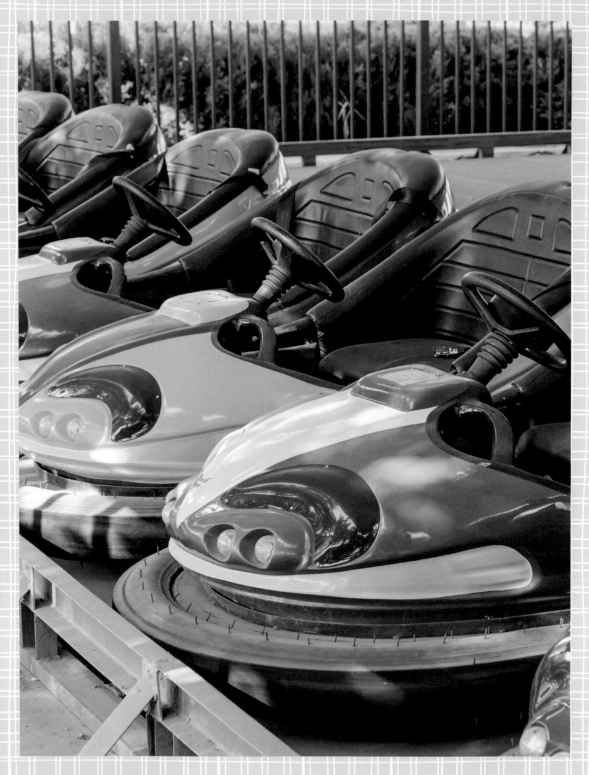

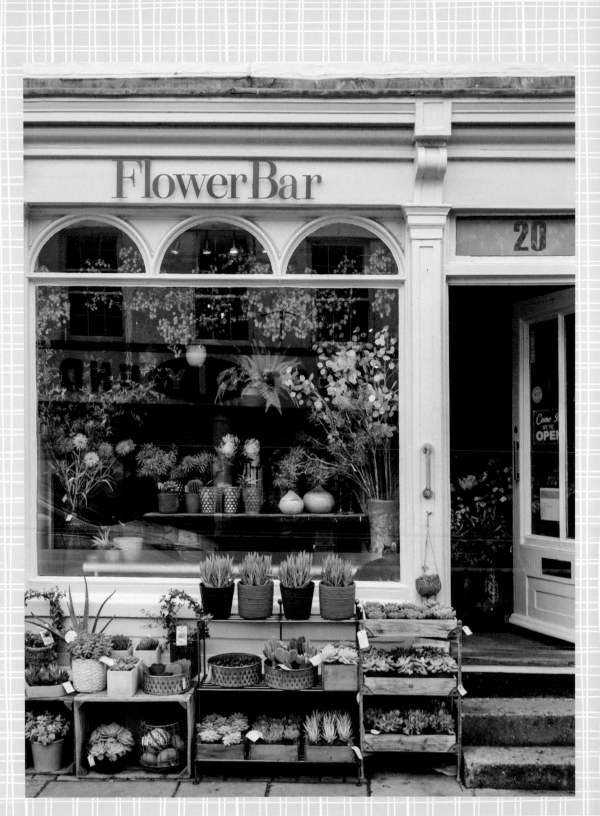

Answer on page 154.

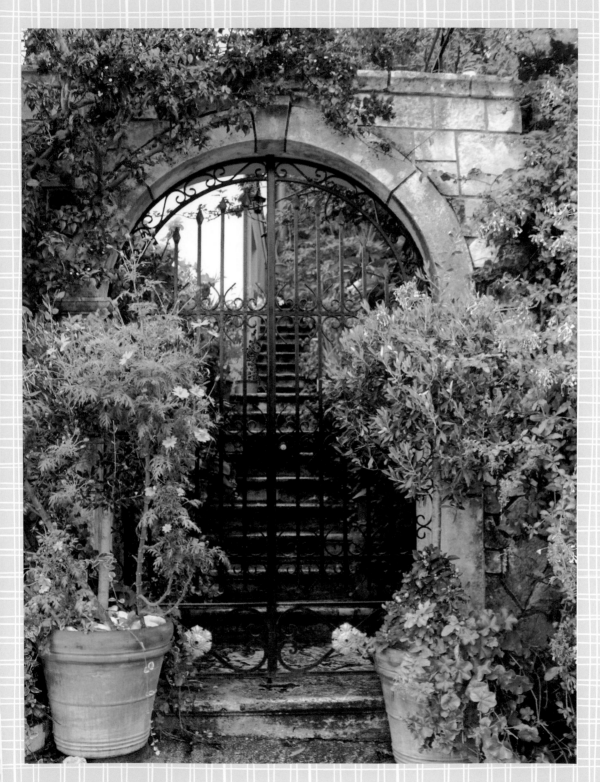

Answer on page 154.

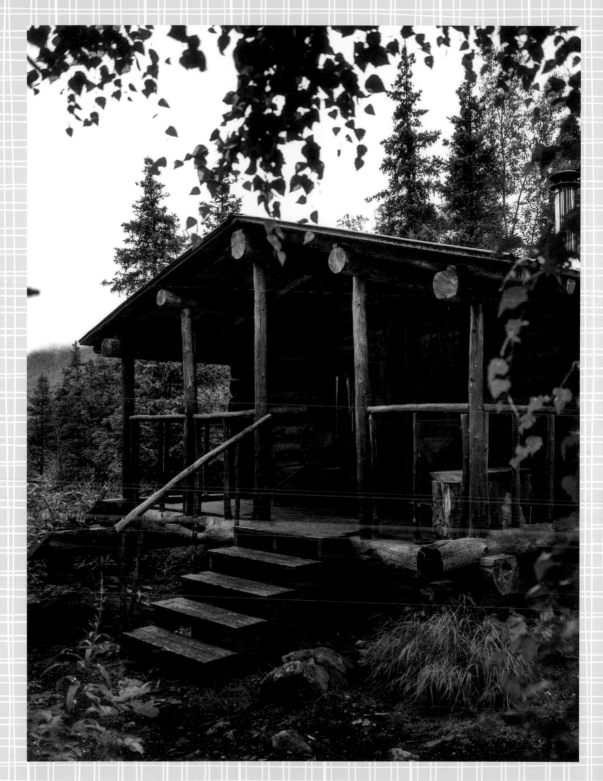

Answer on page 154.

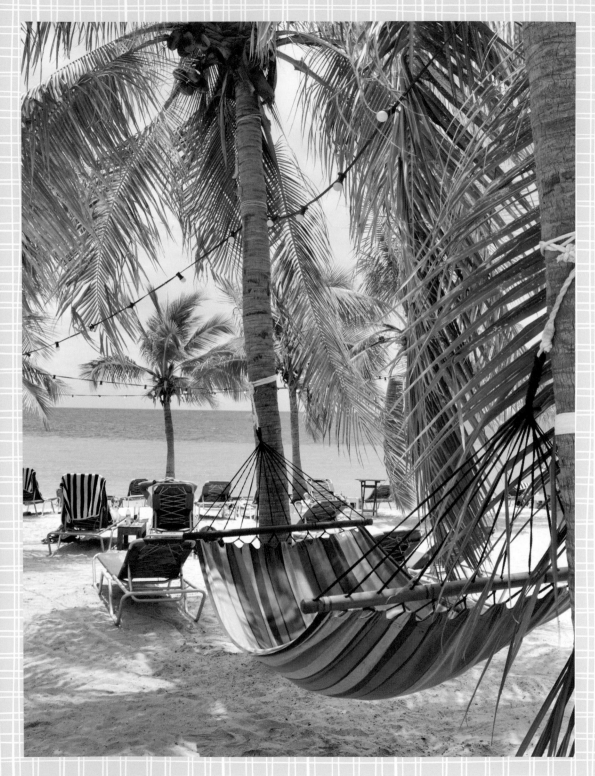

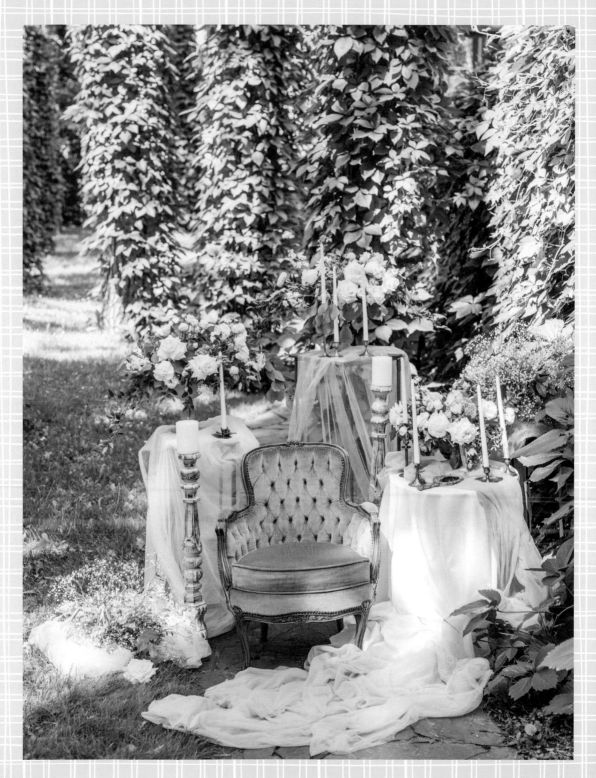

Answer on page 155.

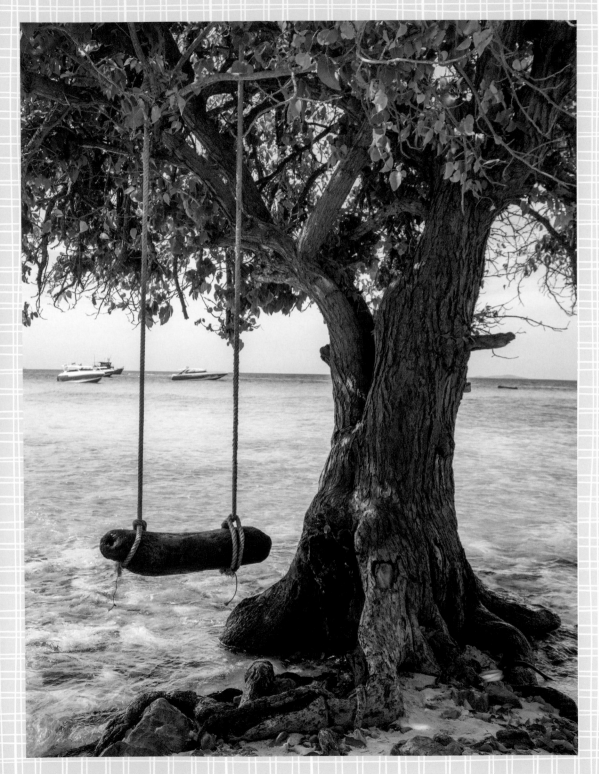

Answer on page 155.

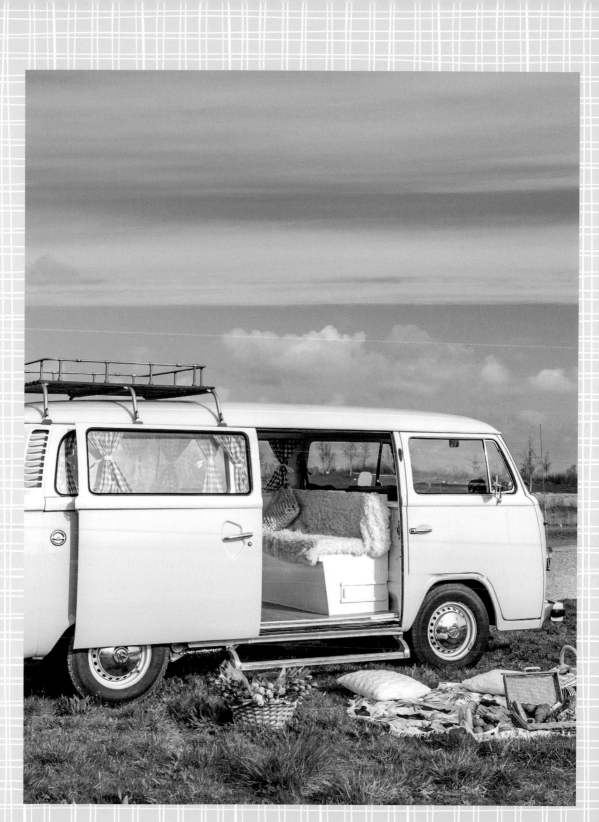

Answer on page 155.

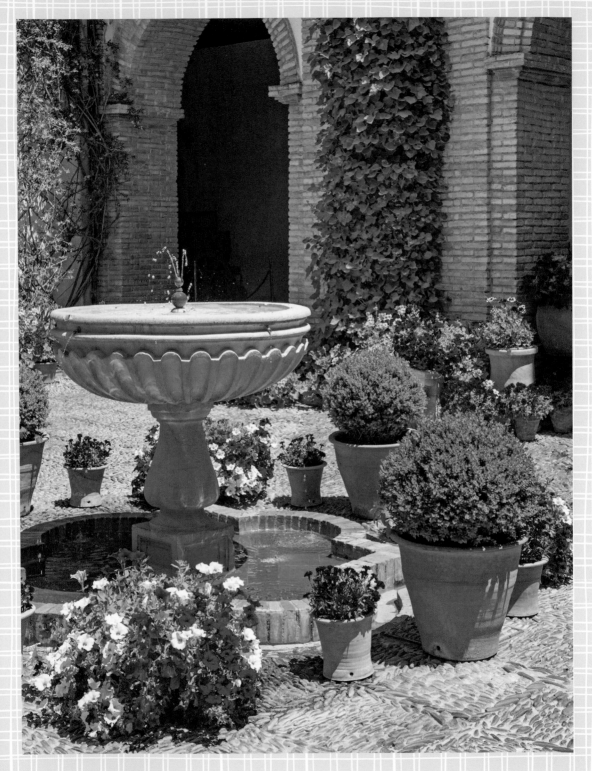

Answer on page 155.

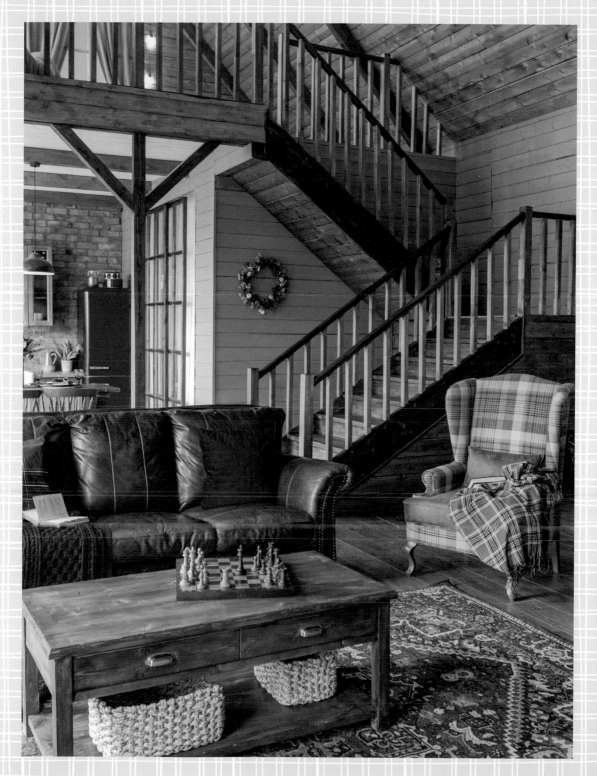

Answer on page 156.

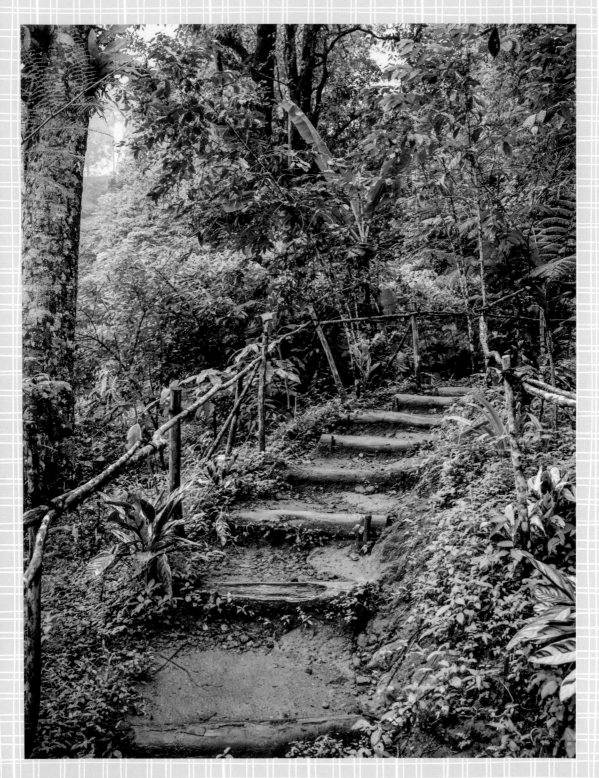

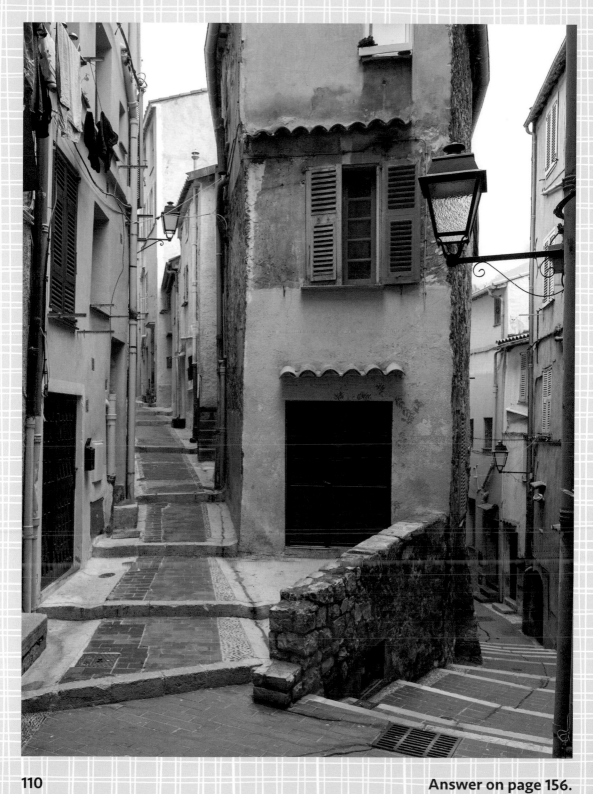

Answer on page 156.

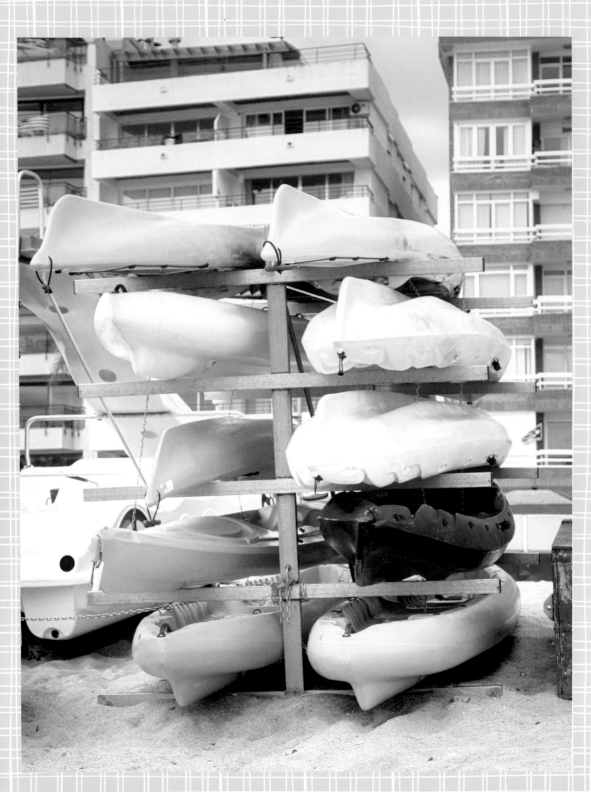

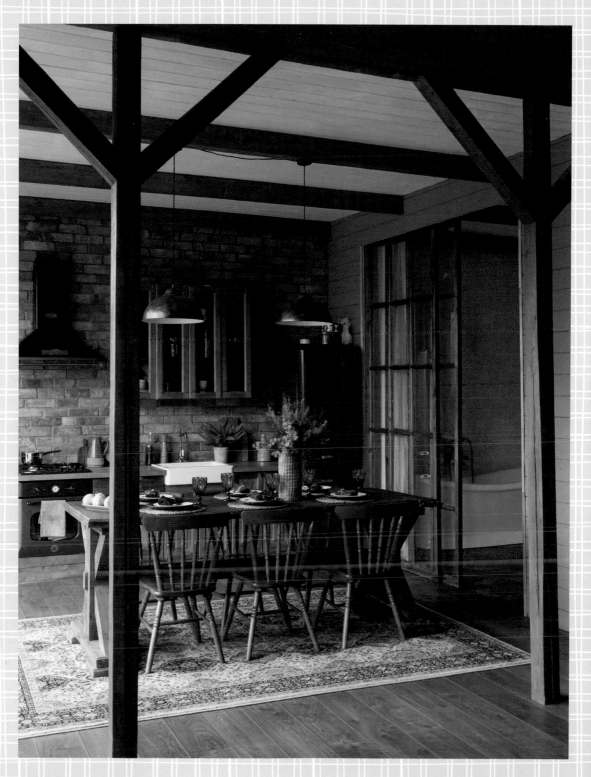

Answer on page 157.

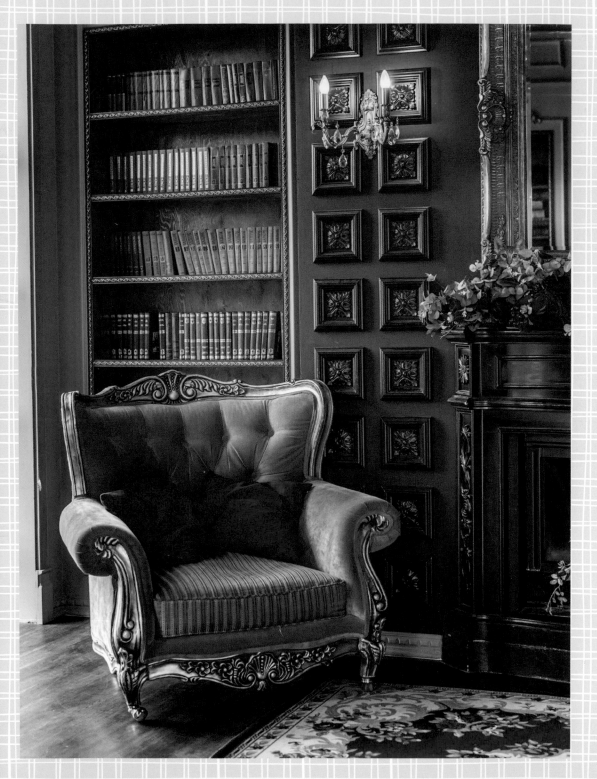

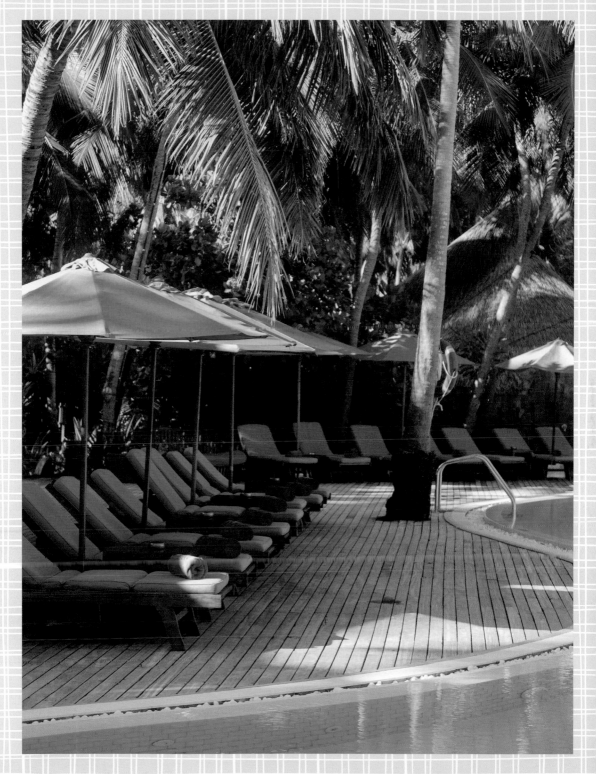

Answer on page 157.

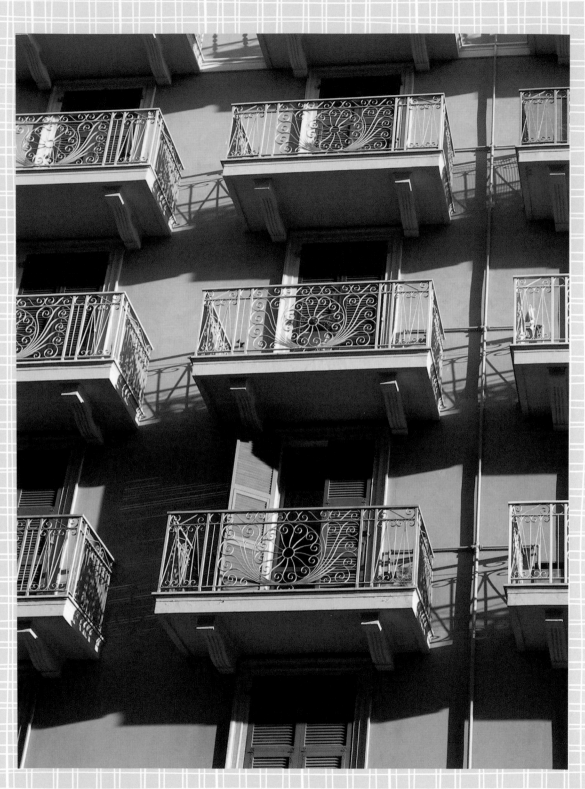

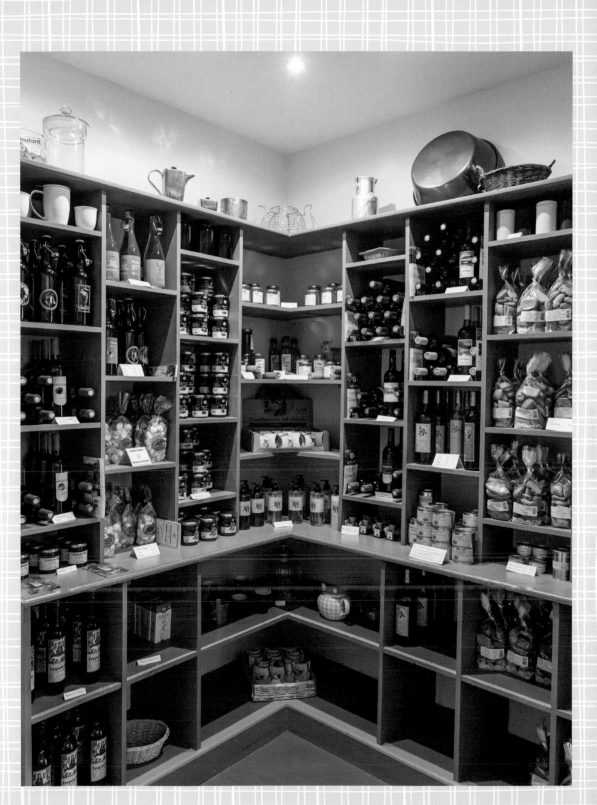

Answer on page 158.

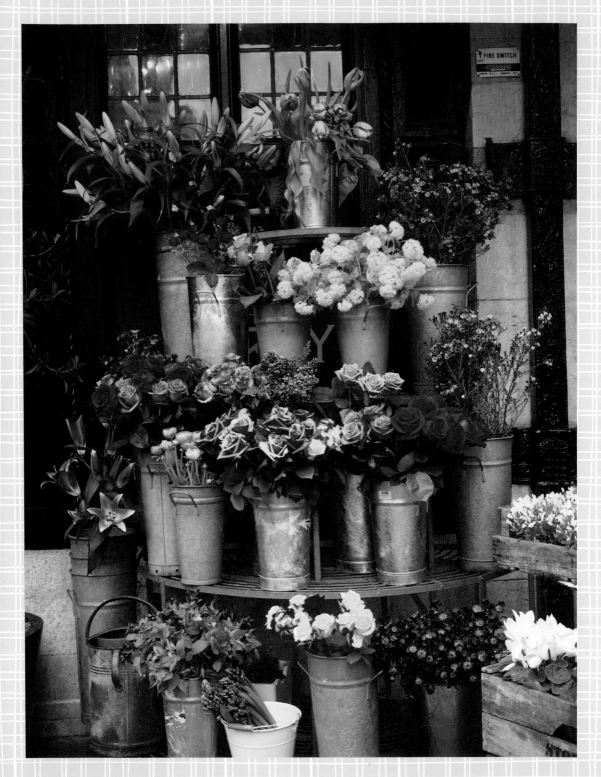

Answer on page 158.

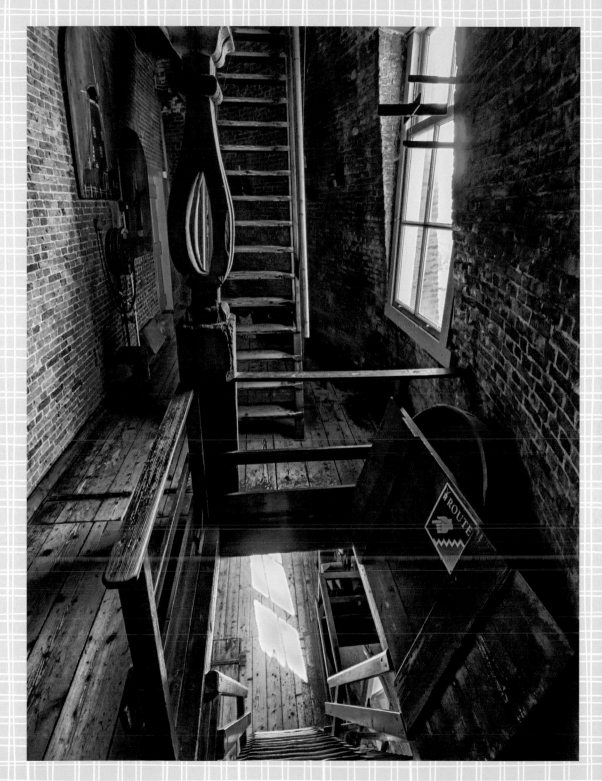

Answer on page 158.

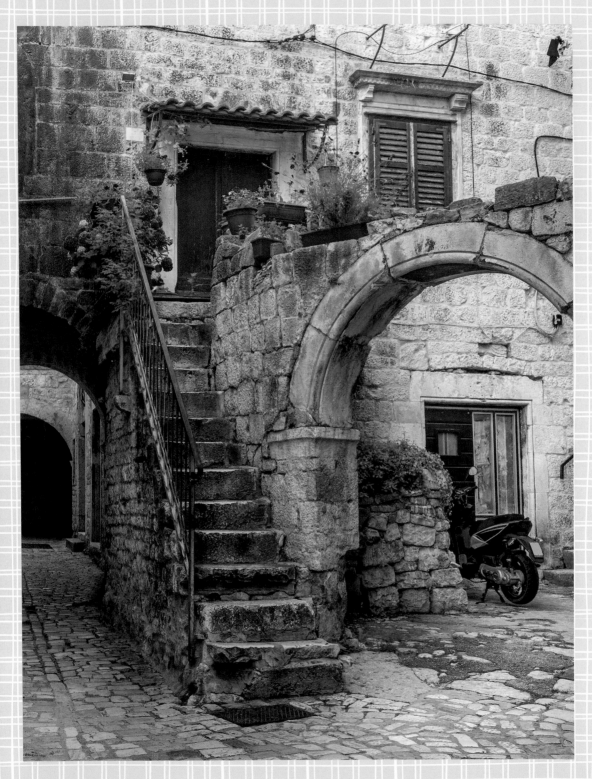

Answer on page 158.

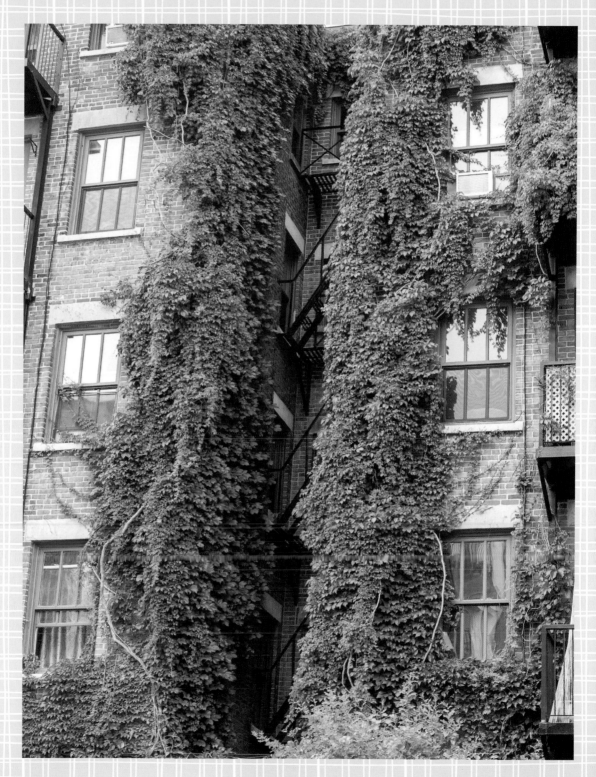

Answer on page 159.

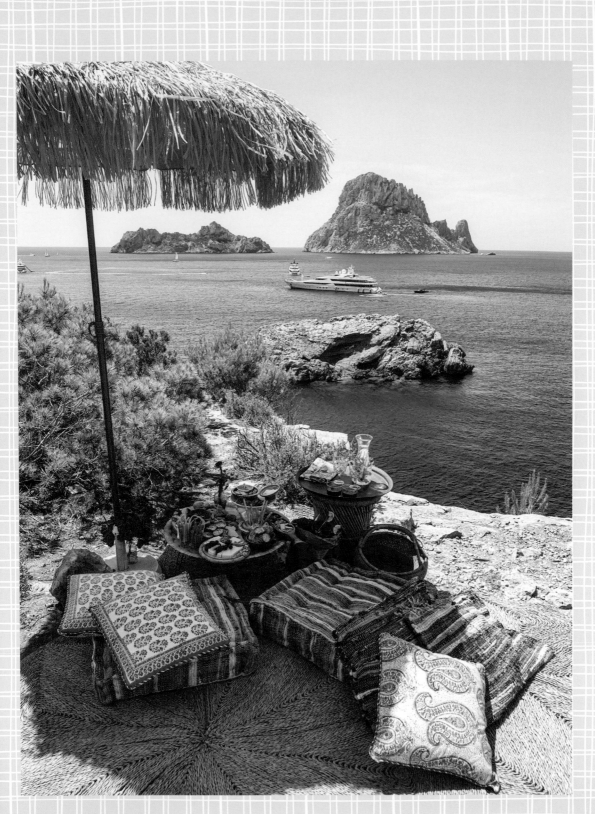

Answer on page 159.

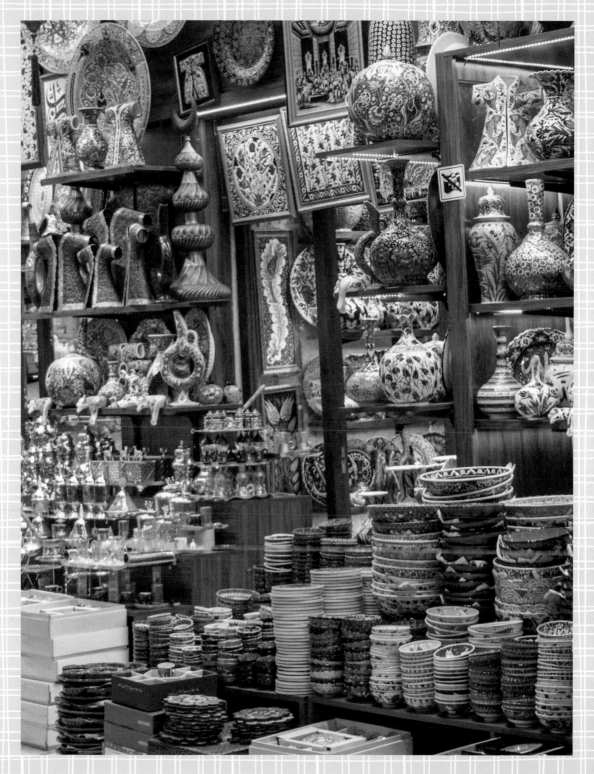

Answer on page 159.

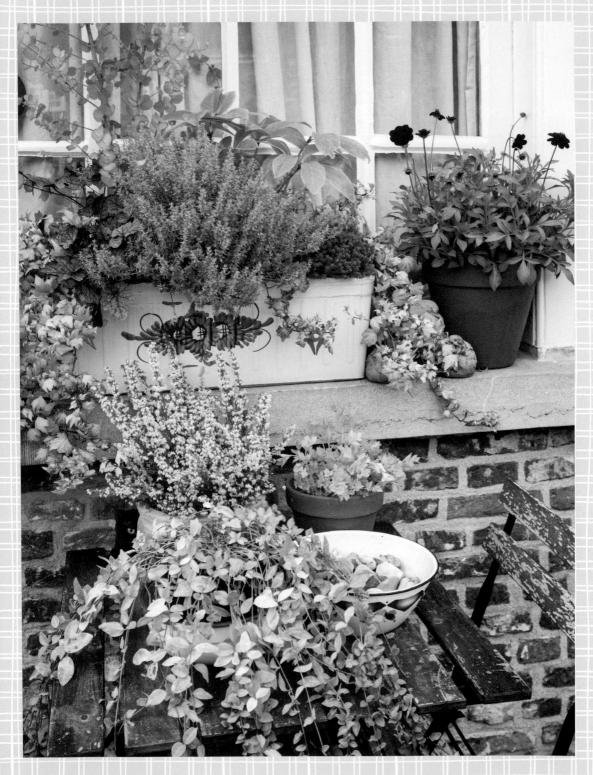

Answer on page 159.

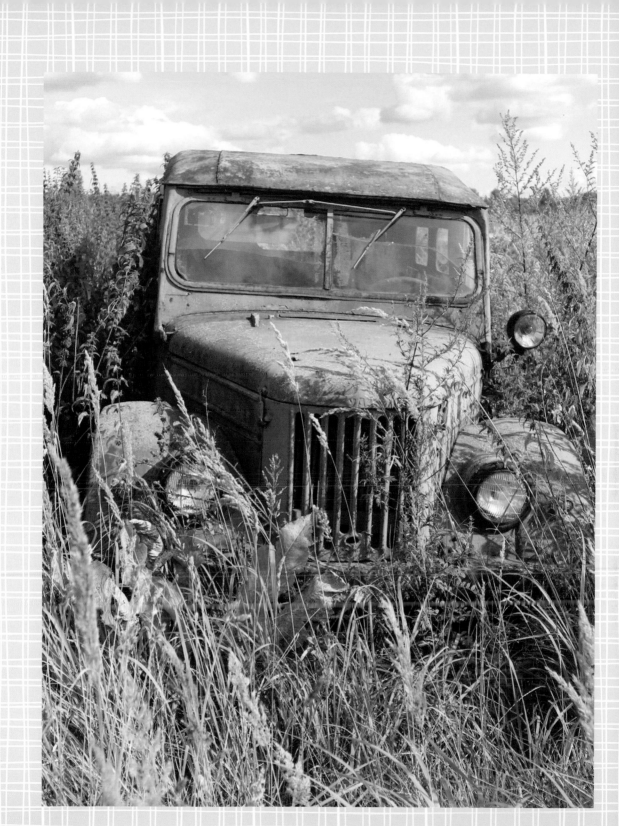

Answer on page 160.

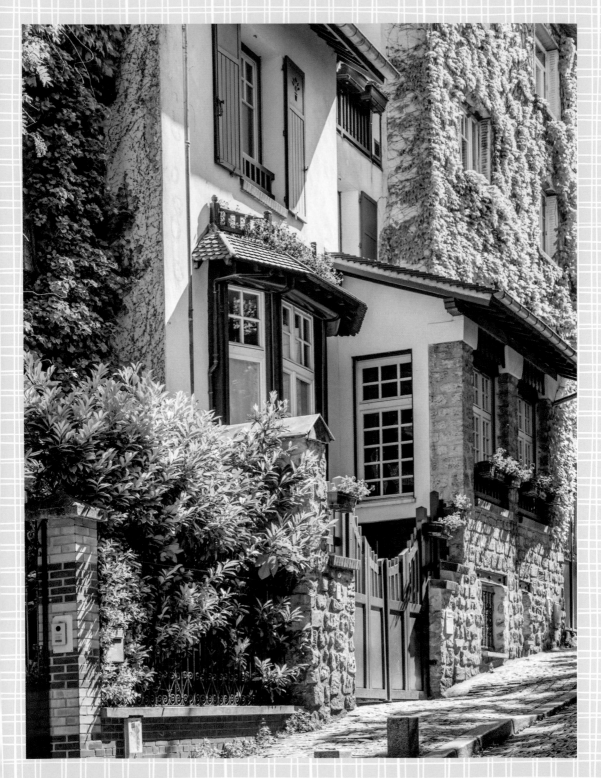

Answer on page 160.

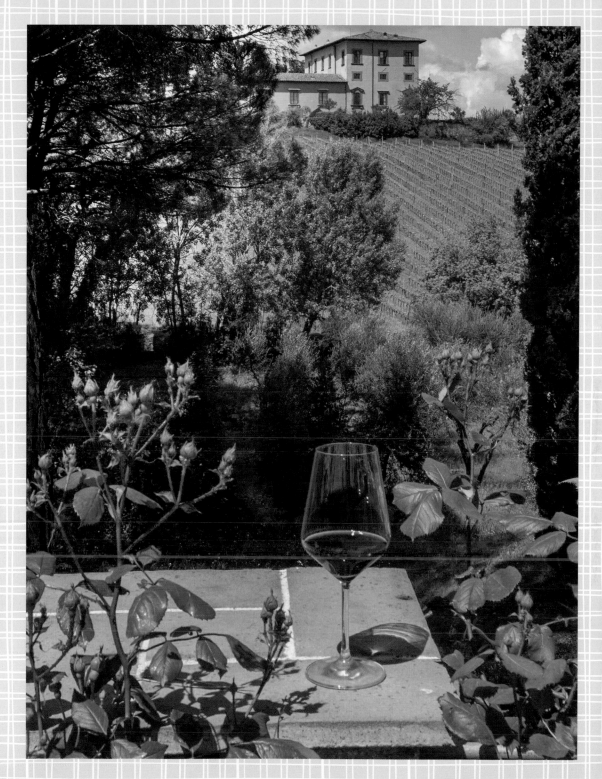

Answer on page 160.

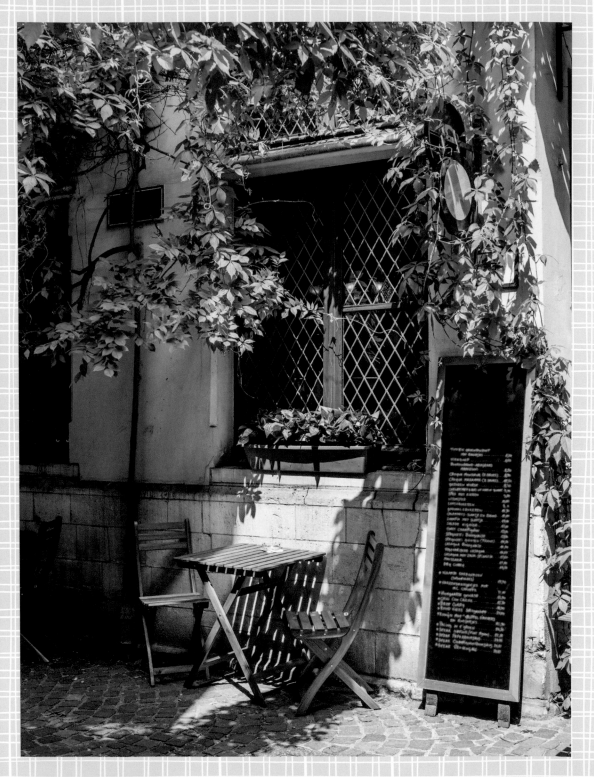

Answer on page 160.

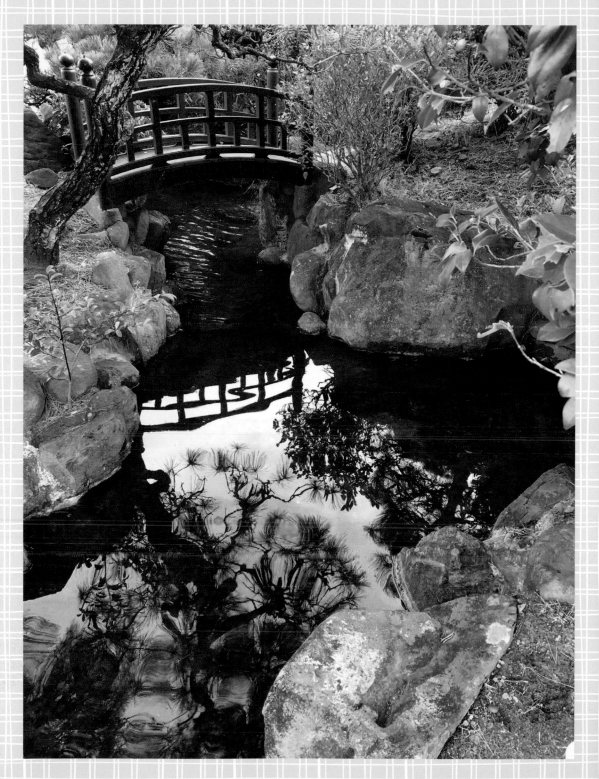

Answer on page 160.

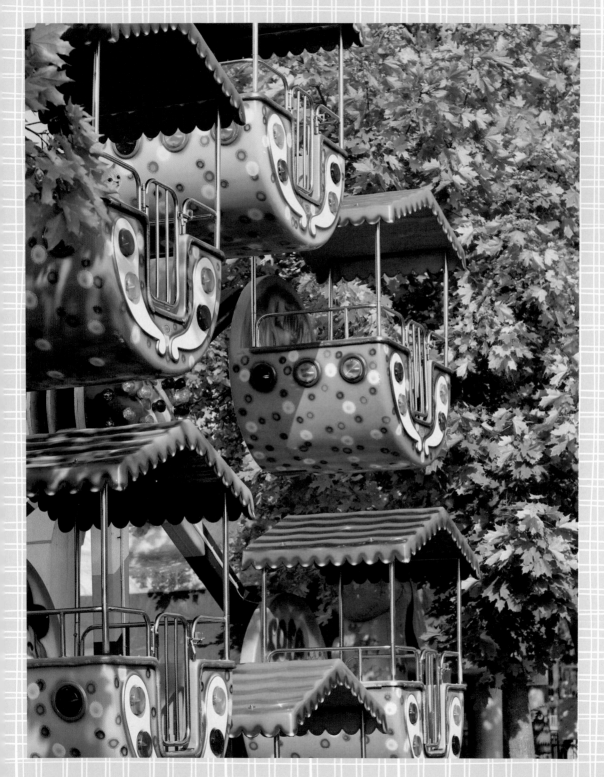

Answer on page 160.

ANSWERS

Page 4

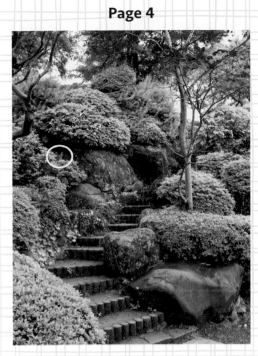

Page 5

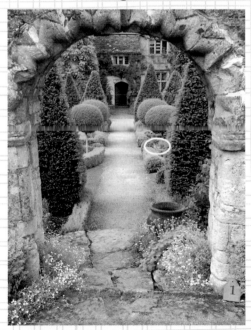

Page 6

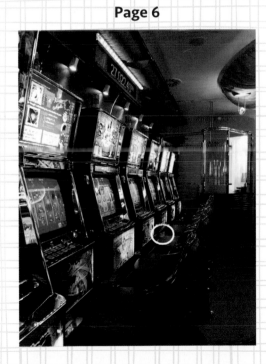

Page 7

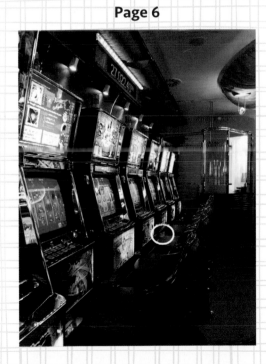

ANSWERS

Page 8

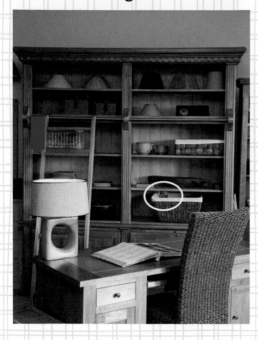

Page 9

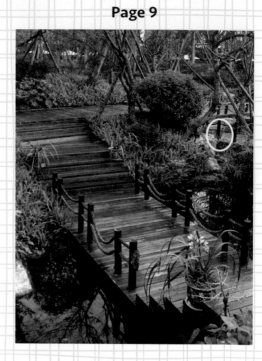

Page 10

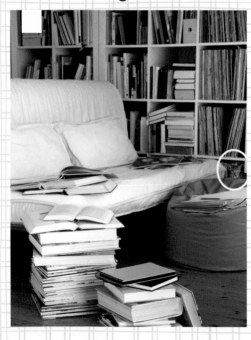

Page 11

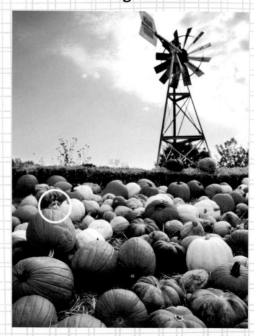

ANSWERS

Page 12

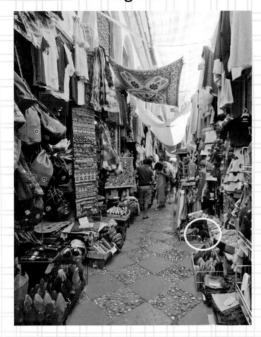

Page 13

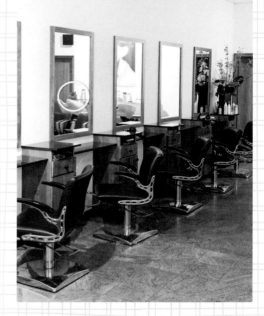

Page 14

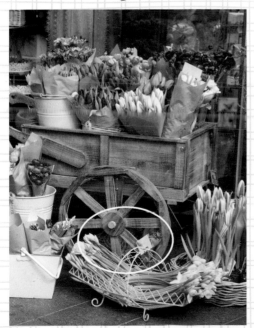

Page 15

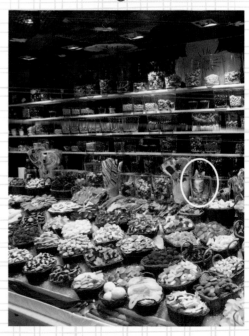

ANSWERS

Page 16

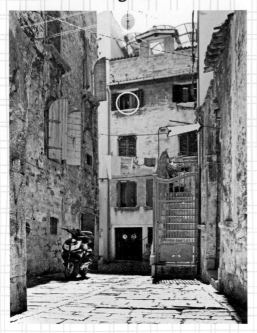

Page 17

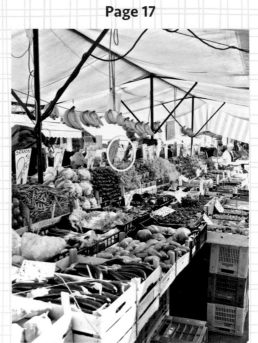

Page 18

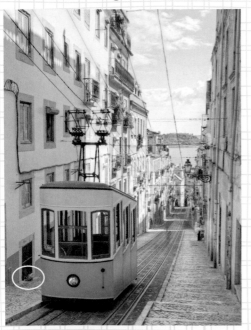

Page 19

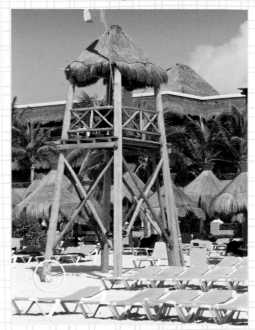

ANSWERS

Page 20

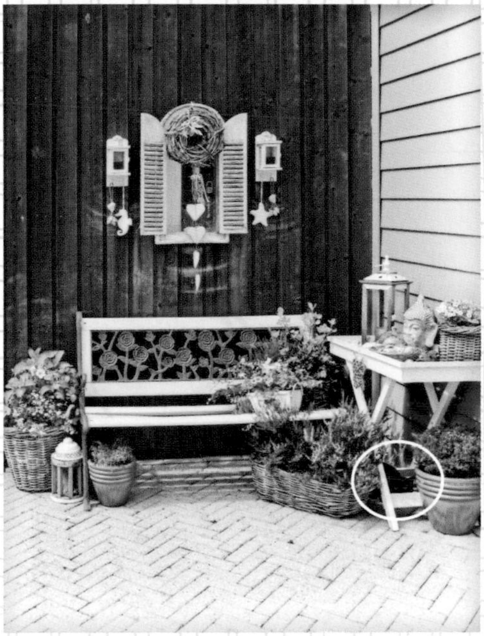

Page 21

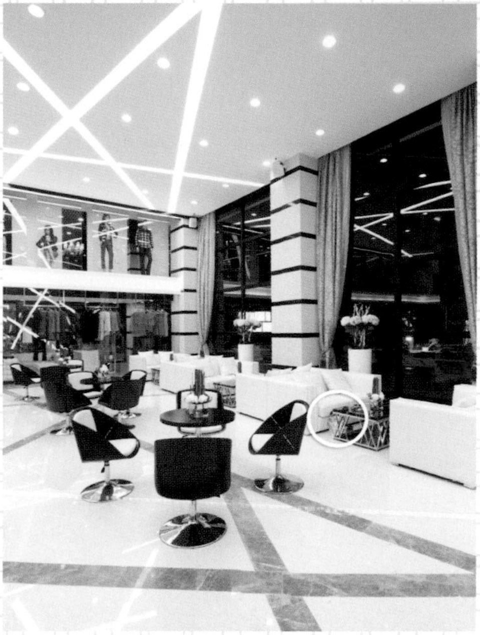

Page 22

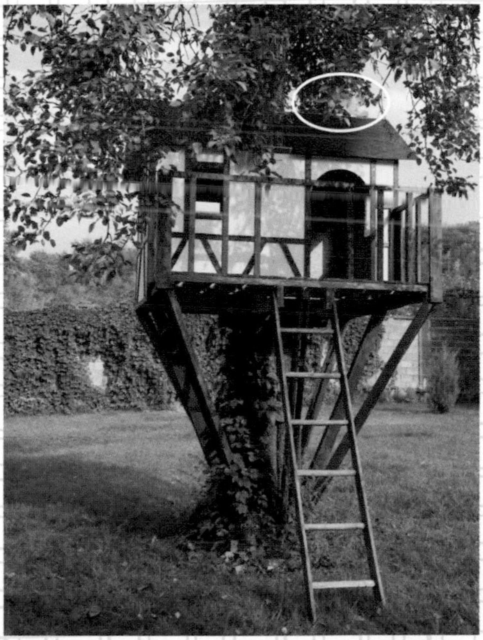

Page 23

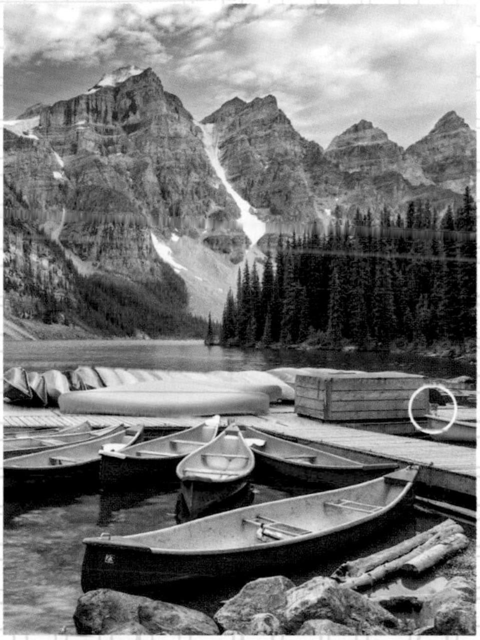

ANSWERS

Page 24

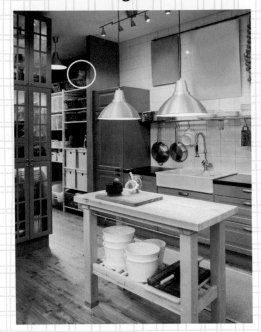

Page 25

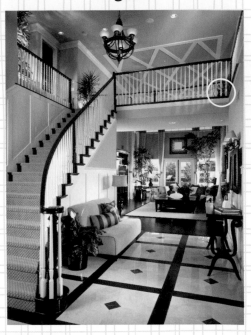

Page 26

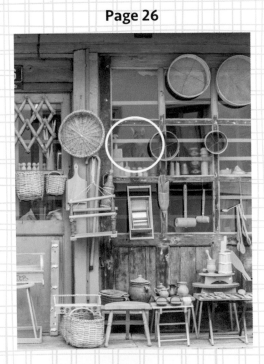

Page 27

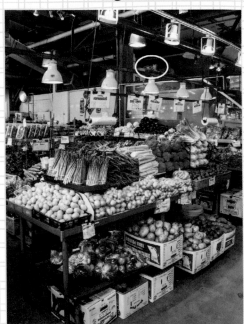

ANSWERS

Page 28

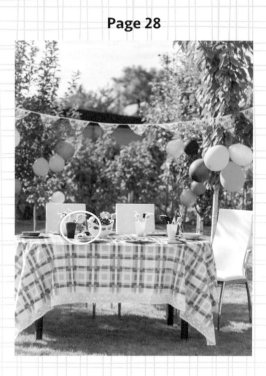

Page 29

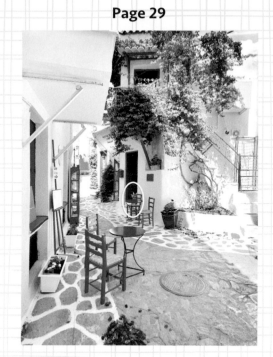

Page 30

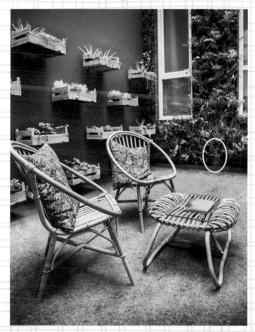

Page 31

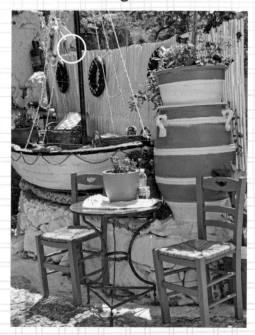

ANSWERS

Page 32

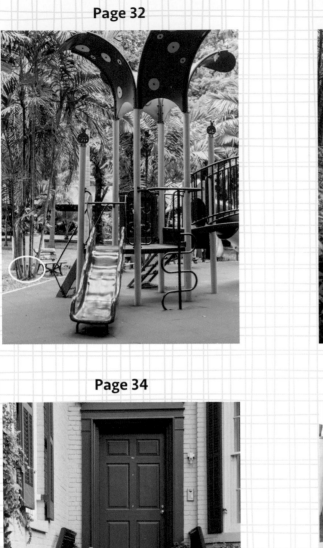

Page 33

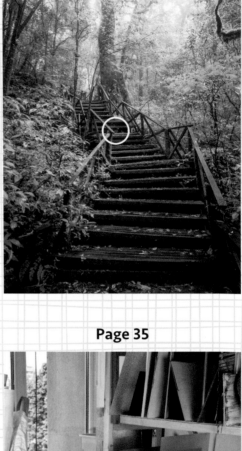

Page 34

Page 35

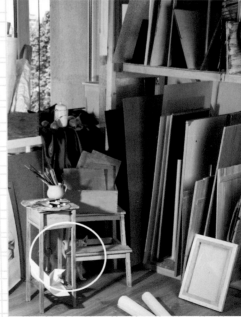

ANSWERS

Page 36

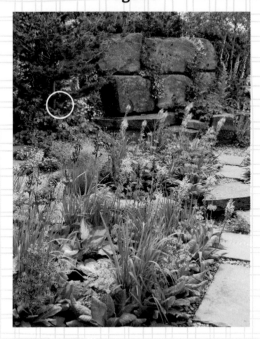

Page 37

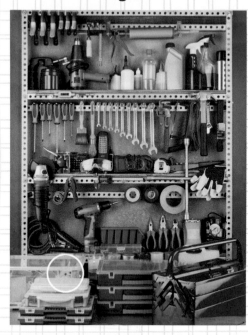

Page 38

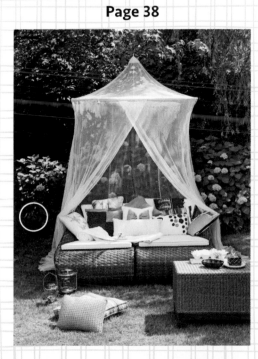

Page 39

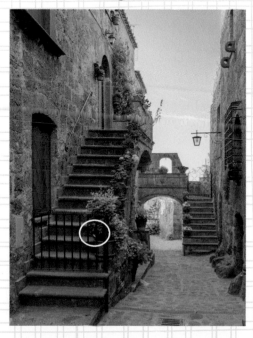

ANSWERS

Page 40

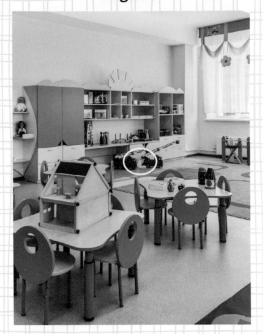

Page 41

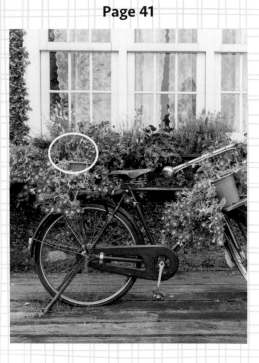

Page 42

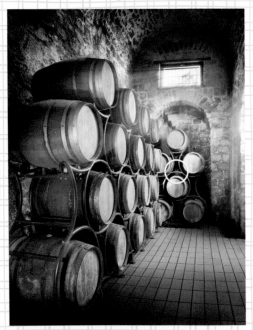

Page 43

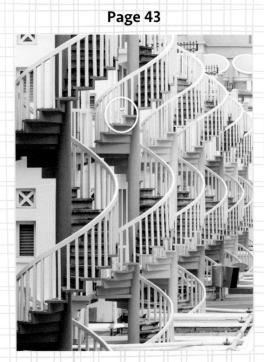

ANSWERS

Page 44

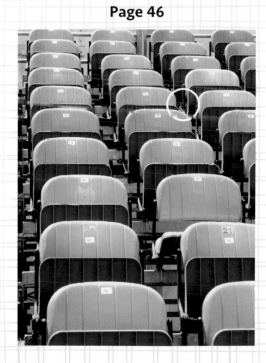

Page 45

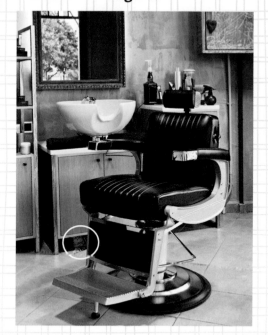

Page 46

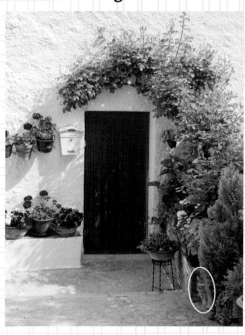

Page 47

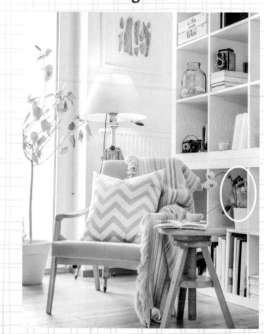

ANSWERS

Page 48

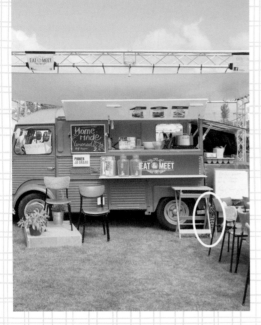

Page 49

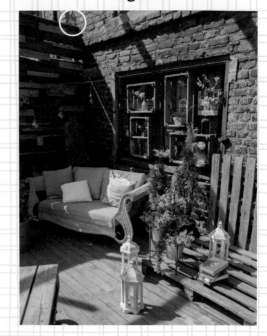

Page 50

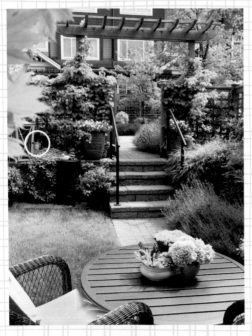

Page 51

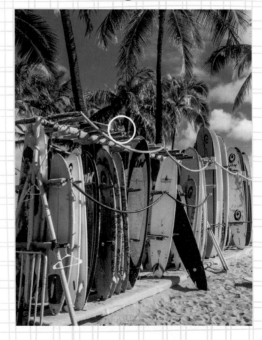

ANSWERS

Page 52

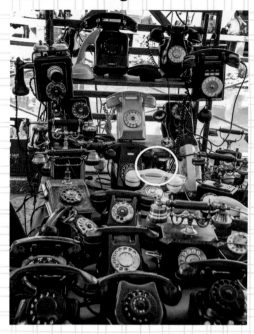

Page 53

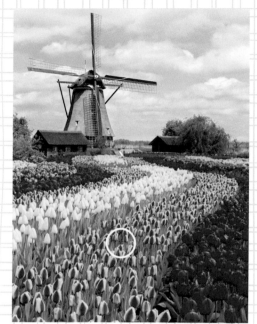

Page 54

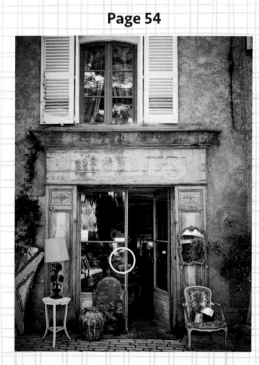

Page 55

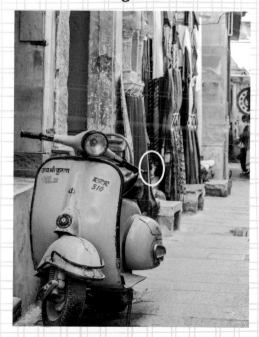

ANSWERS

Page 56

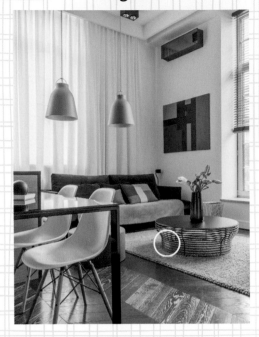

Page 57

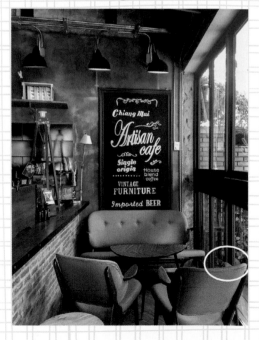

Page 58

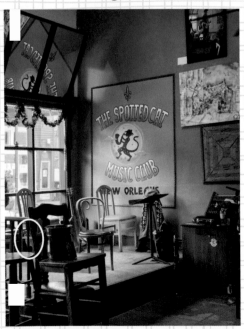

Page 59

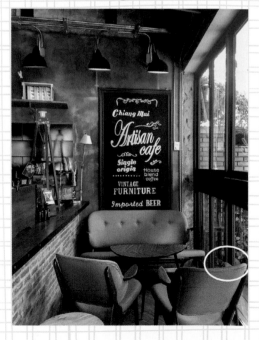

ANSWERS

Page 60

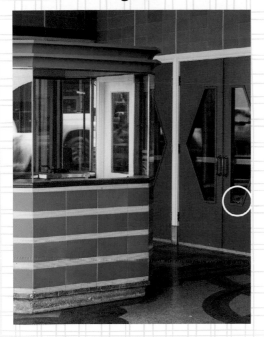

Page 61

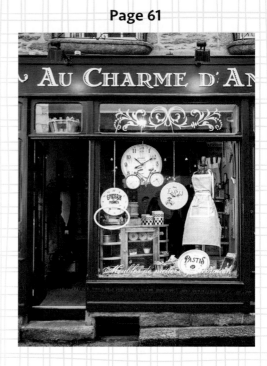

Page 62

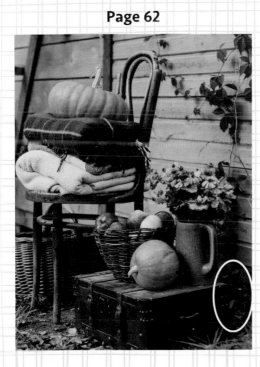

Page 63

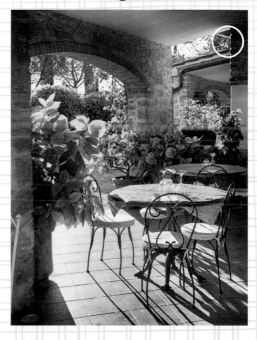

ANSWERS

Page 64

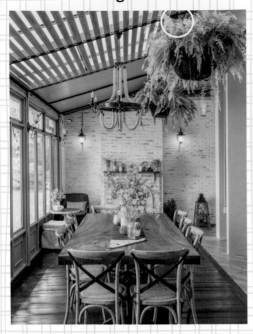

Page 65

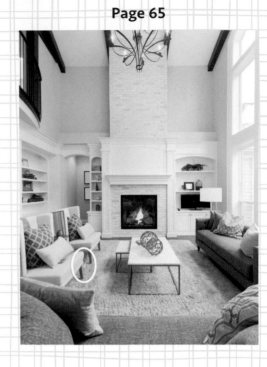

Page 66

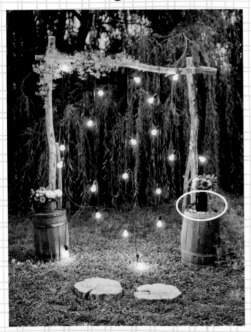

Page 67

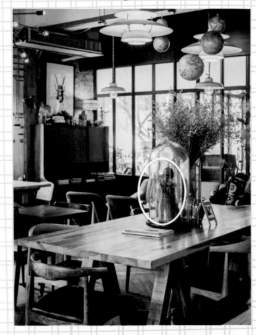

ANSWERS

Page 68

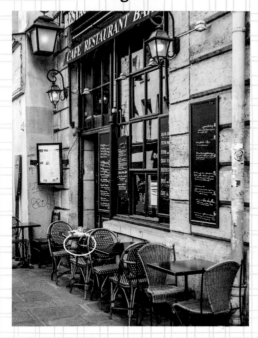

Page 69

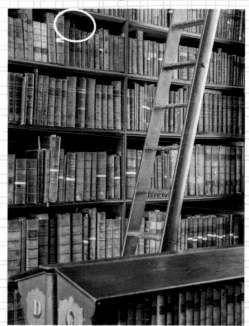

Page 70

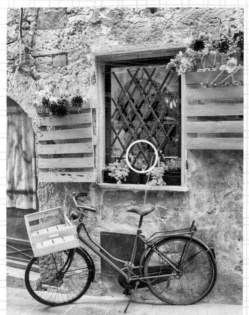

Page 71

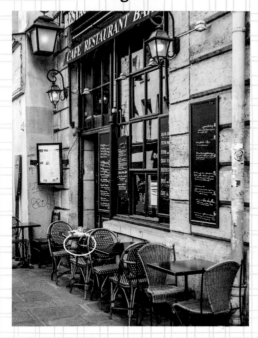

ANSWERS

Page 72

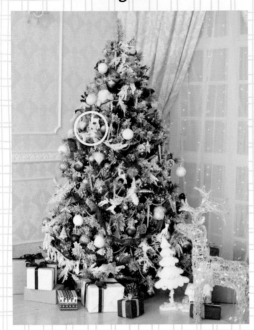

Page 73

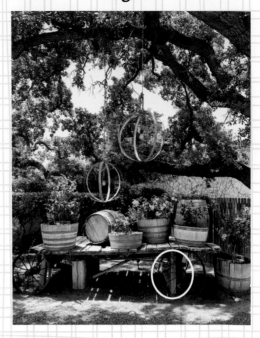

Page 74

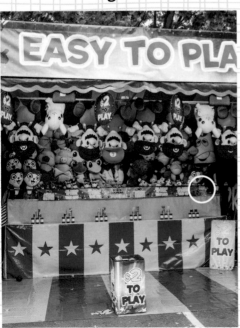

Page 75

ANSWERS

Page 76

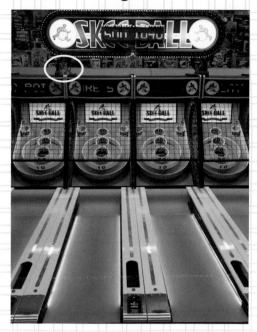

Page 77

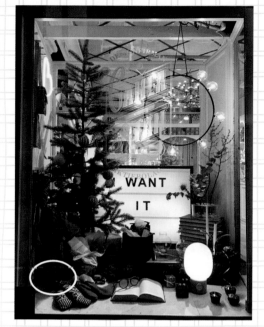

Page 78

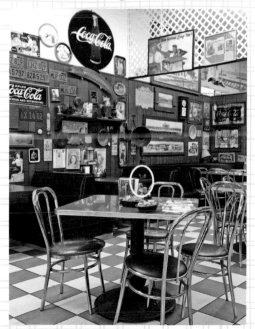

Page 79

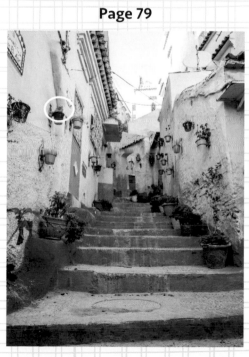

ANSWERS

Page 80

Page 81

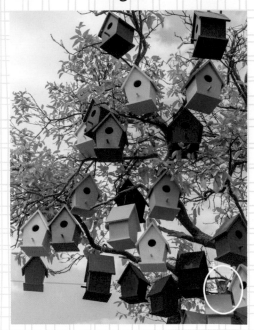

Page 82

Page 83

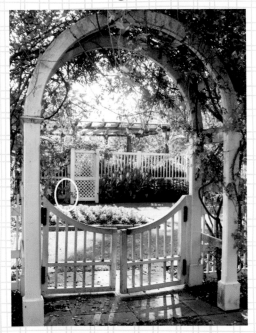

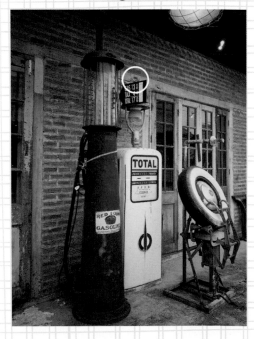

ANSWERS

Page 84

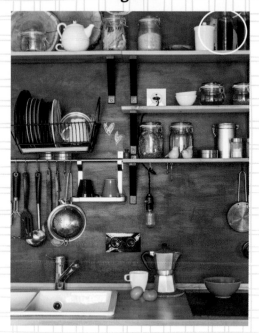

Page 85

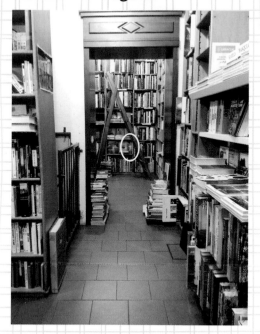

Page 86

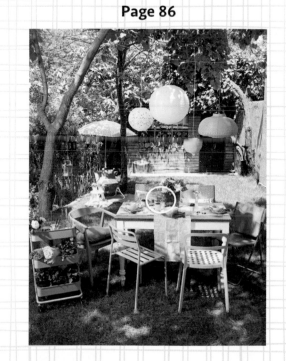

Page 87

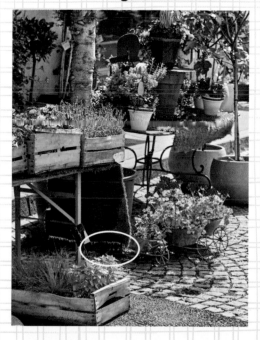

ANSWERS

Page 88

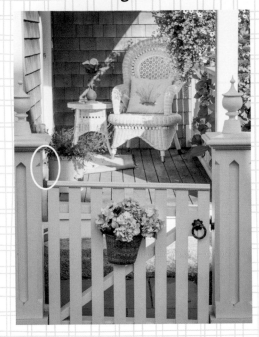

Page 89

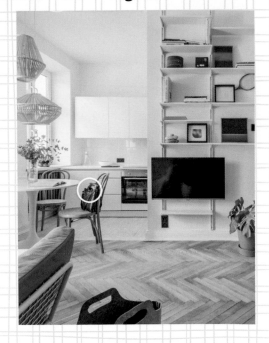

Page 90

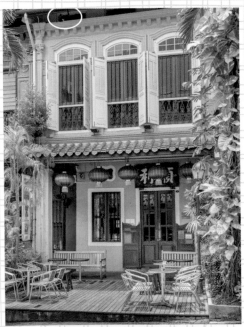

Page 91

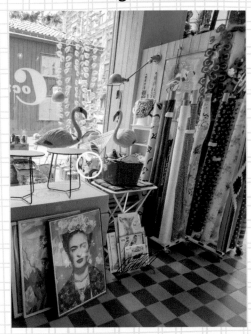

ANSWERS

Page 92

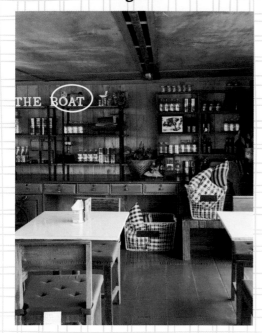

Page 93

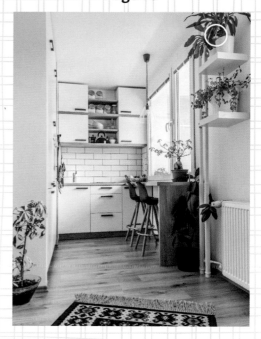

Page 94

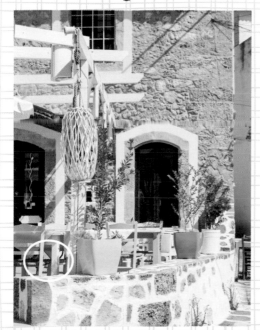

Page 95

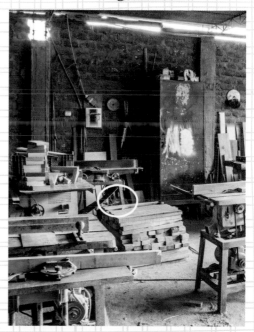

ANSWERS

Page 96

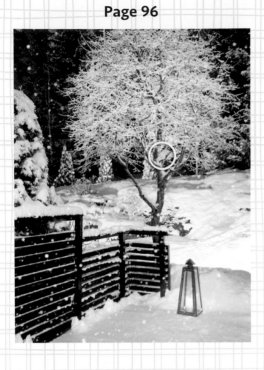

Page 97

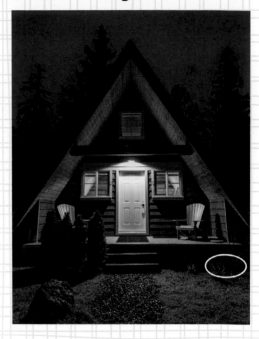

Page 98

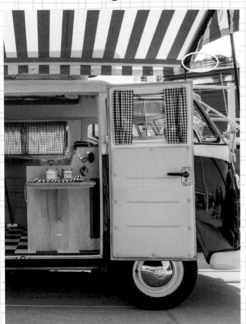

Page 99

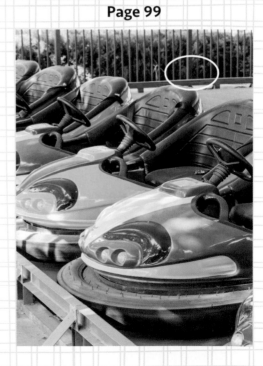

ANSWERS

Page 100

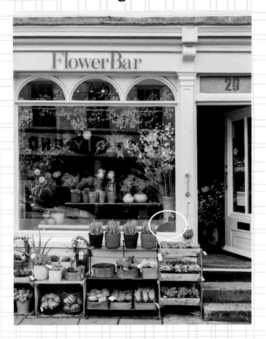

Page 101

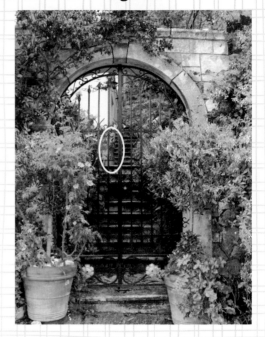

Page 102

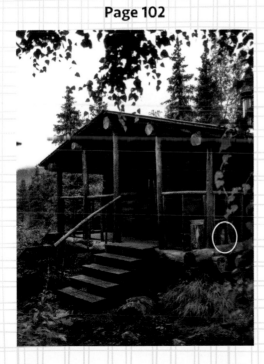

Page 103

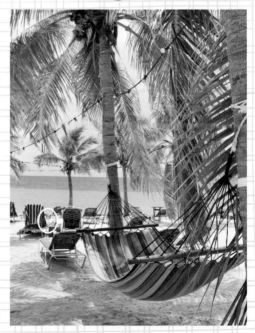

ANSWERS

Page 104

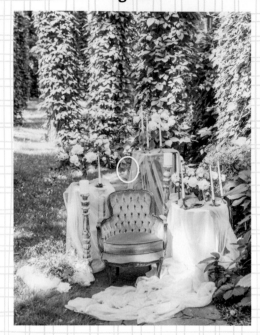

Page 105

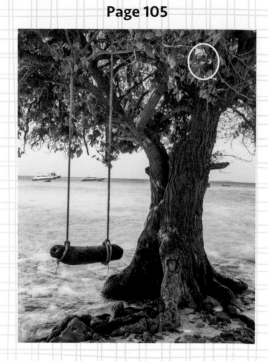

Page 106

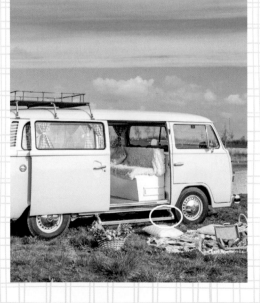

Page 107

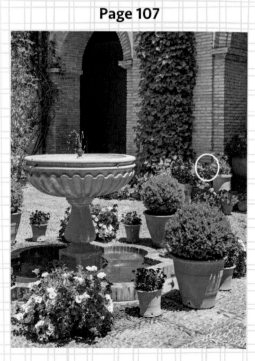

ANSWERS

Page 108

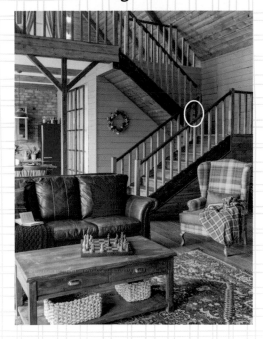

Page 109

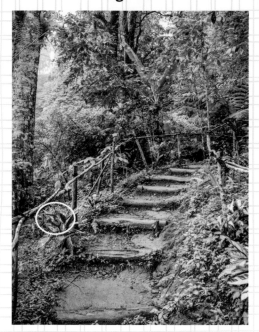

Page 110

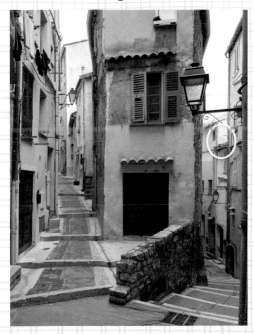

Page 111

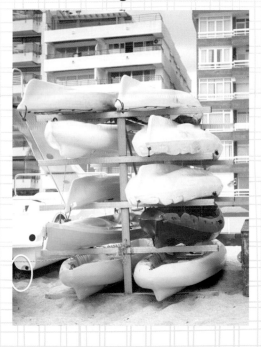

ANSWERS

Page 112

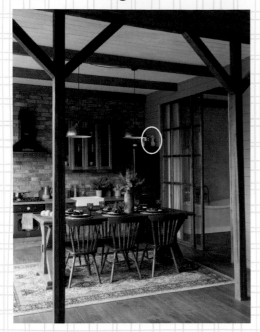

Page 113

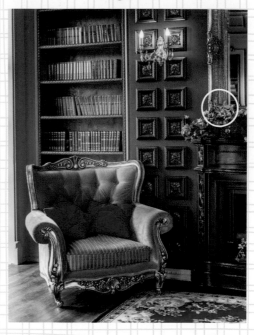

Page 114

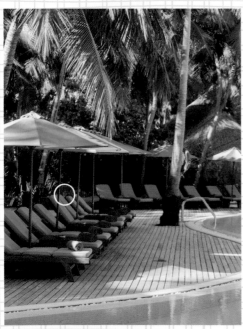

Page 115

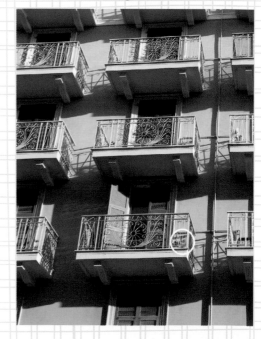

ANSWERS

Page 116

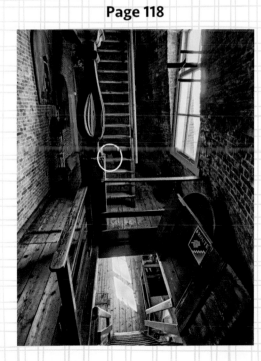

Page 117

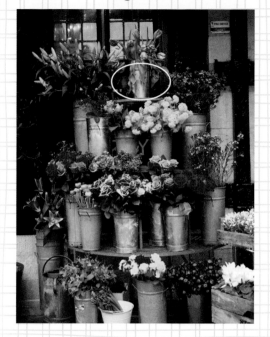

Page 118

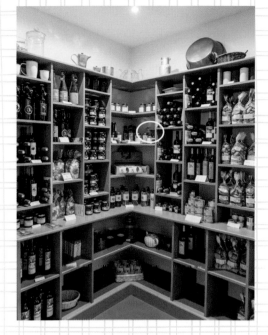

Page 119

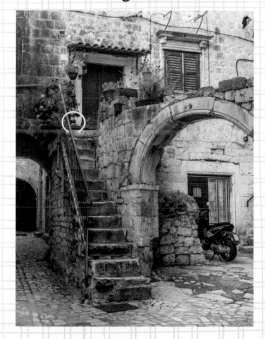

ANSWERS

Page 120

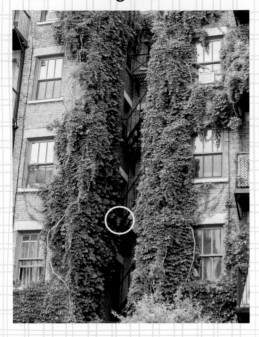

Page 121

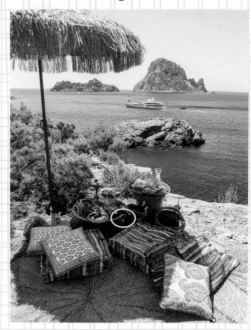

Page 122

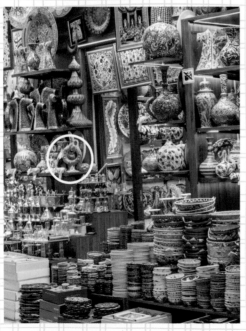

Page 123

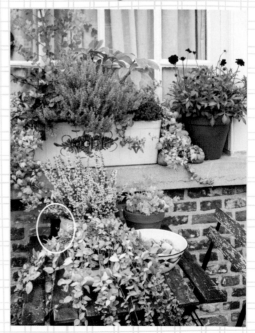

ANSWERS

Page 124

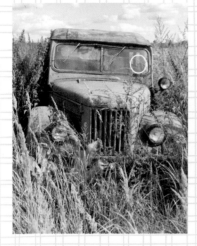

Page 125

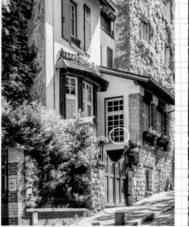

Page 126

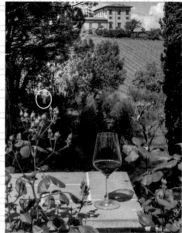

Page 127

Page 128

Page 129

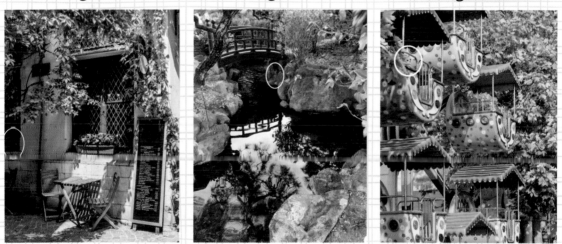

Let's get social!

@Publications_International

@PublicationsInternational

@BrainGames.TM

www.pilbooks.com

BRAIN GAMES

FIND THE CAT CHALLENGE

pil

Publications International, Ltd.

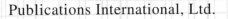